The
DESCENT
of
ELOHIM

HS PRESS

The
DESCENT
of
ELOHIM

Spiritual Messages for the Movie,
The Laws of the Universe
- The Age of Elohim

RYUHO OKAWA

HS Press

Copyright © 2021 by Ryuho Okawa
English translation © Happy Science 2021
Original title: *Elohim no Kourin:*
Eiga Uchu no Ho - Elohim hen *Sankou Reigen*
HS Press is an imprint of IRH Press Co., Ltd.
Tokyo
ISBN 13: 978-1-943928-17-0
ISBN 10: 1-943928-17-7
Cover Image: Toria/shutterstock.com
Annachelnokava/shutterstock.com

Contents

Preface ... 11

CHAPTER ONE
The Descent of Elohim

1. Who Is Elohim?
   - People know the name "Elohim," but not His reality ... 16
   - Starting a spiritual research on Elohim ... 20

2. Why Did Elohim Appear with a Physical Body on Earth? ... 24

3. How Were Earth and Human Beings 150 Million Years Ago? ... 27

4. The Living Environment in the Age of Elohim ... 35

5. Elohim's Power ... 41

6. The Truth of the Space War on Earth ... 45

7. Asking about the Evil God of the Universe ... 57

8. The Meaning of Earth in the Universe ... 60

9   What Did Jesus' Soul Bring to the Earth Civilization? 62

10 The Protector of Elohim 65

11 The Teachings of Elohim 68

CHAPTER TWO

A Spiritual Message from Elohim
—Elohim and His Age—

1 The Age of Elohim and What Happened After That
   The risk for the souls to be born in a physical body 74
   The beginning of hell 78
   The origin of devils and the establishment of hell 82
   The two ways to clean out hellish values 85

2 The Formation of Hell and the Dark Side of the Universe
   What human beings are tested to see 88
   When human beings lose qualification as children of God 91
   The true nature of the souls of Jesus, Michael, and Amaterasu-O-Mikami 94
   A route connecting hells between planets 97
   The reason light of angels need to be born one after another 100

3 The Danger in "Democracy without God" and "Freedom without God" 104

CHAPTER THREE

Lyrics of the Original Songs for the Movie, *The Laws of the Universe - The Age of Elohim*

"Elohim's Theme" 110

"Panguru's Theme" 114

"Jesus of the Beginning" 116

"Yaizael's Theme" 120

"The Miracle of You" 124

"The Fallen Angel's Theme" 126

Afterword   129

About the Author	131
What Is El Cantare?	132
What Is a Spiritual Message?	134
About Happy Science	138
About Happiness Realization Party	142
Happy Science Academy Junior and Senior High School	143
Happy Science University	144
Contact Information	146
About IRH Press	148
Books by Ryuho Okawa	149
Music by Ryuho Okawa	159

Preface

Throughout history of this earthly world, there has been a clash of value between the faith in the only God and the faith in many gods, sometimes causing religious wars.

This book is the answer for it.

El Cantare, the God of the Earth, descended to this world as "Alpha" over 300 million years ago and carried out His mission as the Creator God. He descended for the second time as "Elohim" and indicated good and evil, justice, and mercy.

The movie to be released this autumn, *The Laws of the Universe - The Age of Elohim*, depicts the age of Elohim. It was a beautiful age, but it was also a time of test for Earth. The name "Elohim" also appears in the Old Testament, so Jewish, Christian, and Muslim people know it. However, no one knows what Elohim looked like and what His age was like. For this reason, we decided to publish this book as the reference material for the original story of the movie, prior to its release.

Ryuho Okawa
Master & CEO of Happy Science Group
August 21, 2021

CHAPTER ONE

The Descent of Elohim

*Originally recorded in Japanese on December 29, 2016
at the Special Lecture Hall of Happy Science in Japan
and later translated into English.*

Elohim

One of the core consciousnesses of El Cantare, the Supreme God of the Earth Spirit Group. He descended to the region presently known as the Near and Middle East 150 million years ago, when the world now known as hell was beginning to form in the lower part of the spirit world. To guide people in the right direction, Elohim taught mainly on the difference between light and darkness, and between good and evil. "Elohim" means "Light" or "Light of God."

*The Descent of Elohim: Spiritual Messages for the Movie,
The Laws of the Universe - The Age of Elohim*

1
Who Is Elohim?

People know the name "Elohim," but not His reality

RYUHO OKAWA

Today, we will record a spiritual message from Elohim, titled, "The Descent of Elohim."

This is for our next movie. The previous movies, *The Laws of the Universe - Part 0* was about five high school students fighting against evil aliens, and Part 1 was a story centering around Alpha. I'm considering making the next one, Part 2, centering around Elohim. But since there are almost no firsthand material on Elohim, I think it will be very difficult to make Part 2. So, we need to make as many firsthand sources as possible. We have talked about Elohim several times before, so there is some information, but I don't think it is enough.

Elohim is not necessarily fiction. The name is known in reality. The fact is that people don't know the truth about Elohim. Happy Science teaches that Alpha is one of the core consciousnesses of El Cantare who was born about 300 million years ago and Elohim was another who was born about 150 million years ago.

It is known, for example, by scholars who study the literature on the Old Testament, that there are two gods that the prophets believe in, and that there is a difference between them. It is said that there are two kinds of literature on the Old Testament; one is called the Yahwist source, while the other the Elohist source. The former depicts a god of anger, jealousy, and judgment, or a god who is too ethnic. However, the god that the latter depicts seems somewhat different from the god of the Yahwist source. The Elohist source has documents that show a different image of God, which would lead to the religion of love preached by Jesus Christ later on. So, opinions seem to be divided over whether this is really one God or not.

Also, according to our teachings, the God that the Jews believed in, called Yahweh or Jehovah, is different in nature from the God that Jesus believed in. I have once mentioned that Jesus was persecuted and crucified partially because of his lack of awareness; he confused two gods of different nature and perceived them as one God. In addition to that, we said that Elohim's character appears quite strongly in Allah, the one and only God that people in the Middle East believe in. Some of our space people readings describe what Elohim looked like, but I don't think they are credible enough yet.

There is a movie series called *X-MEN* about the battles of mutants who have supernatural powers. One of the series was released in 2016 and I recall watching it during my flight to New York. It was the Chinese version, so I'm not sure if I understood it well enough, but the name Elohim clearly appeared in the movie and he was depicted as the very first mutant like the X-Men. I don't remember exactly, but the story is probably set around 5,600 years ago in the Middle East—actually, it suggests an area closer to Egypt. It is set in the desert region around the ancient time when pyramids and mummies were first created. In the movie, Elohim is like a priest and a psychic, and he absorbs more and more energy from other psychics and magnifies himself to become bigger and more powerful. I don't think he is depicted as a 100 percent good being; rather, he is portrayed as a god of destruction. He comes back to life in the present day, but he's so powerful that it takes about 10 X-Men to take him on. The movie does not depict him in a good way and I felt that a bad image of Elohim spread around the world because of the Hollywood movie, or from the "Hollywood source."

After watching the movie, I felt that the image of Elohim in *X-MEN* overlapped with that of Osiris, or as we call him, Ophealis, the ancient Egyptian king. When Ophealis was killed, he was dismembered, but later, his body parts were gathered and wrapped in bandages like mummies, and he was resurrected. After that, (according to Egyptian myths) Osiris became the king of the underworld. So, the filmmakers' image of Elohim may overlap with that.

In this way, although people know the name "Elohim," His reality is unclear. In such a situation, it would be difficult for us to get information that is credible.

Starting a spiritual research on Elohim

RYUHO OKAWA

We still have plenty of time (until the release of the movie), so today, we will just try to get firsthand information that will help us create some pictures or a story for Part 2 of *The Laws of the Universe*, in which Elohim appears. Since there are no other material available, I would like to go ahead and record a spiritual message from Elohim without considering what I have already mentioned about Him. For now, I'm aiming to reach the level where we can develop the movie's plot.

Alpha and Elohim are described as beings in the ninth-dimensional world, or the so-called world of saviors, but they are much different from the other guiding spirits in the ninth dimension. I feel they are one step higher than the ninth-dimensional spirits who have a strong human side to them or who strongly show aspects as gods with human character. Alpha and Elohim are more like beings who express a consciousness of the tenth dimension or higher. Otherwise, it would be impossible for them to be involved in a big plan like the Creation of Earth. The so-called ninth-dimensional spirits are personified gods that are born on earth every 2,000 to 3,000 years to create cultures and civilizations or to save humanity. But the core consciousnesses of El Cantare are involved in larger issues like the plans for Earth and the universe.

I have said many things (about Elohim) before, but today, please leave them aside. I would like you (the interviewer) to ask questions for our movie. You can completely ignore the audience and ask whatever you want to know to make the movie, even if the answers may not come out as a teaching as a whole. If we aren't able to ask everything we need, we will have to try again on another day. And we will also need to collect supporting evidence from other spirits who have a connection to Elohim.

As for the scale of time, 150 million years is beyond your comprehension. The Elohim in the aforementioned movie *X-MEN* lived around 5,600 years ago, which is fairly recent. That was, at oldest, the early days of the Egyptian civilization. This is in the range of what you can understand. From the point of view of modern-day common sense, it is believed that the present human race appeared around 30,000 to 50,000 years ago, or at most around 100,000 years ago. Some theories go back as far as a million years and sometimes we hear about the fossils that look like the remains of human beings from around five million years ago. But if we go back as far as 150 million years, even archaeologists cannot say for sure. There is a limit to what can be discovered by digging in the ground. We cannot dig up the entire surface of Earth and we cannot find out what is submerged under the sea. And I don't think the surface of Earth was the same as it is now. So, I will ignore the archaeological or scientific point of view and try to research as much as I can spiritually. There might be some information that will be hard to believe in terms of the oldness of the times, but since most religions contain some cultural symbols, I believe there are some truths in symbolic terms that we must understand.

Elohim we will talk to today is not a fictional being. His name has been known since ancient times in religions, especially in those that are the source of Christianity and Islam. However, we don't really know what kind of God Elohim is. So, we want to get an idea of His outline and tendencies.

I don't want my reasoning to get in His way. I think it would have been better if I were a little drunk [*laughs*]. It would be better if I were a little more relaxed, but for now, I would like to give it a try as it is and leave it to you (the interviewer) to lead the session.

Now, I would like to summon Elohim, one of the core consciousnesses of El Cantare, who is said to have come down to this world after Alpha (the first core consciousness to do so), and ask questions about His time, activities, and thoughts.

The Spirit of Elohim, the Spirit of Elohim,
The Spirit of Elohim.
Please come down to Happy Science
And tell us about your appearance,
Thoughts, and actions
In a way that we can understand.
The Spirit of Elohim, the Spirit of Elohim.
Please teach us about your thoughts,
Teachings, and activities.
Thank you very much.

[*About 15 seconds of silence.*]

2
Why Did Elohim Appear with a Physical Body on Earth?

ELOHIM

Hmm.

INTERVIEWER

Thank you very much for coming down here today. How were the earthlings like when you were alive?

ELOHIM

In Alpha's time, His focus was on creation, so His teachings had an aspect of "be fruitful and multiply and fill the earth." In that sense, the main idea was to let people with different characteristics try to live on Earth. Gradually, it became necessary to develop a civilization that was unique to Earth, and it was no longer possible to leave it as diverse as it was.

There were opinions over what kind of lifestyle or existences should or should not be accepted on Earth. It means there was a need to make a distinction between good and evil. The confusion was not caused by Earth-born beings only. Space people who later became the ancestors of human beings were coming to Earth from various places. Each planet, star system, or galaxy had its own values, which somewhat conflicted with each other, so there were many clashes between what each of them thought was justice. So, it became very important for us to choose what we thought was right and wrong on Earth. We can say that when we started to clearly discern between good and evil, the spirit world began to be divided between the so-called heaven and hell.

So, as is the case in your world as well, there were people that you just couldn't get along with. In such a case, you need to live separately like the horizontally divided companies. This is one way, and in reality, people were divided into many countries and ethnic groups. The other way was to be divided vertically. It was necessary to distinguish between what was desirable and what was undesirable on Earth, beyond differences in ethnicity, skin color, and appearance. At that time, a kind of boundary was beginning to form in the spirit world, preventing some spirits from going up above a certain level, though it was not yet called hell. It would be similar to the high-class and low-class areas in modern society. Some spirits could go to the higher realms of the spirit world that had the image of the mountainous area—a symbol of the heavenly world—while others remained in the realm that had the image of the ground surface, or in a realm where spirits could avoid being seen by others. These realms were beginning to form.

This was why I needed to appear with a physical body on earth to show people the standard to tell good from evil.

# 3
How Were Earth and Human Beings 150 Million Years Ago?

INTERVIEWER

Please teach us what races or species were thriving back then.

ELOHIM

Hmm. [*About 10 seconds of silence.*]

First, the reptilians were dividing into two major kinds. The ones that degenerated became like dinosaurs and increased in brutality. With the food on Earth... At that time, also because of gravity, they tended to be huge and many turned into dinosaur-like beings. Others maintained human-like characteristics strongly. But they tended to seek sacrifices or tried to secure their own prosperity at the price of others, and became the ancestors of humans with such a tendency. These creatures have become what are now called ogres, demons, or the type of spirits who transform themselves into aggressive animals or monsters.

They are ancestors to such beings. If not ogres, they became beings like Dracula or man-eaters who would arouse some kind of fear in others. I think these two kinds of reptilians mainly caused confusion.

But other beings also had a lot of difficulty in adapting themselves to the earthly environment. Earth was quite different from the home planets of many space people, so they could not live on Earth as they were. That is why some tried to crossbreed themselves with Earth-born humanoids and create a physical body that was suitable to Earth.

While they still had a foothold on Earth as space people, they had to crossbreed with some earthlings—which is still done even today by some aliens—and modify their bodies to adapt to Earth's gravity, percentage of oxygen and other components, temperature, and soil and water. It means they re-created their physical bodies to suit Earth's environment. They surely possessed highly advanced technology, but if they retained the technology they brought from their planets, they would end up dying inside the spaceship. So, they modified their bodies to live on earth. This required quite some trial and error.

When traveling in space, their life span was unclear because traveling at a speed faster than the speed of light made it hard to tell how many Earth years they had lived. However, being born on Earth and experiencing Earth's revolution of 365 days per year gave them a sense of time. So, they were able to calculate how long they could live based on the Earth time.

At the time, everything was primitive, like a newly founded company or military where people have not received enough education or training. So, people clashed with each other and caused confusion often.

INTERVIEWER
Please tell us about the dominant reptilian races and types, their characteristics, and their detailed appearances at the time.

ELOHIM
The ones relatively closer to humans were probably similar in form to modern people's general image of "aliens" from outer space. They gradually changed form after some time, but that was their basic prototype. The ones that

became animals changed that way due to the food they ate. Also, there were still many that could fly. The ones that flew, ones that submerged underwater, and ones that were mainly on land changed their form accordingly. They were the prototypes of various living things today, so they were also the common ancestors.

The huge creatures no longer exist and I think this is due to the change in food situation. Today, global warming has become an issue, but back then Earth was a little warmer than it is now. It wasn't uninhabitable. When it's warmer, living beings tend to grow larger. Food becomes abundant and animals that were preyed on grow larger as well. So, the predator grows even larger. Today, Japanese carps only become as large as one meter (about three feet), but if you bring them to Thailand, they can grow as large as three meters. So, when the prey grow larger and the temperature rises, the predators tend to become larger. At that time, it was warmer than now, or more like the tropical region, so most beings were generally larger.

It means smaller creatures were always exposed to danger, so they needed to protect themselves. They acquired the ability to move more swiftly or faster, or the ability to hide themselves such as by digging themselves in or diving in the water to escape from their enemy. These quick reflexes became necessary, and they also developed higher intelligence than their enemies, so that they could protect themselves by predicting how their enemy would attack them. Actually, in the process of their becoming humans, they developed a lot of wisdom to protect themselves from fierce animals or dinosaur-like creatures, in other words, the wisdom to overcome fear.

However, among those who died in fear, there were quite many that couldn't return peacefully to the heavenly world. Here lies the beginning of hell as a lower spirit world. In most cases, I think it began with chagrin or discontent of those who had desired to live in this world but was killed by vicious predators or larger creatures. Those beings started to dwell there and created collective thoughts. This occurred in different parts of Earth and eventually, there came a new leader in hell.

INTERVIEWER

There are various types of reptilians such as those that submerge, fly in the air, and more. Can you teach us their colors and physical attributes as well?

ELOHIM

Most of them had the color that would allow them to blend into their surrounding environment. Their body was green if they lived in lots of greenery, soil color if mainly near dirt, and close to the color of swamp if they lived in swampy areas. Of course, among those living in the ocean, there were those with blue bodies. There was also the opposite case; some had colors that stood out to show off their strength. They had vividly contrasting colors from their surroundings to show that they were superior in their abilities or functions, and put others off eating them. They were trying to show their strength by taking on primary colors or colors different from the natural environment.

In addition to these, there were also those who had the body color of red, yellow, or orange to show that they were poisonous if eaten. Even today, for example, mushrooms with vivid colors tend to be highly poisonous. This is warning that if you eat them, you will die. Among the living creatures were strongly poisonous ones if eaten, similar to the puffer fish today; the predators that eat them will die by poisoning. These creatures took on a very colorful appearance to show they are different from other prey. They protected themselves by having very vivid colors in this way.

The creatures that became the base of animals that live today mostly existed during my time, although they were a little larger and had harder skin, scale, or shell to protect their bodies. Many of these creatures that were heavy with strong protection became extinct during an age later than ours, when Earth turned into a desert and then cooled down. Some of the creatures that became smaller could survive, which ushered in an era of mammals. Some say this happened because of a huge meteor that crashed into Earth. Anyway, eventually, an era began where huge creatures could not survive, but in my time, such huge beings still existed.

After all, among the creatures that were created, there were those with more protective functions, more attacking abilities, or even more poison than animals today. There were those that were poisonous when eaten, those that gave off poisonous gases, and those that oozed poisonous liquid as if they were sweating. Take a frog, for example. There were much bigger ones back then and when they were attacked, they would change colors, form some kind of warts, and when the attacker tried to bite, the warts burst and gave off poison that would instantly paralyze the predator. There were creatures similar to the gentle hippopotamus we see today, except some of them would emit poison from their nose. They became smaller, and the prototype of something like a boar appeared, but some of them could still emit poison to protect themselves.

As for humans, of course, many of them had no fur from the beginning, so naturally they needed something to cover and protect themselves from enemies. Even so, because it was relatively warm, they did not need the kind of clothing like the ones you wear today. It was just minimum clothing. Still, there were some humans that wore bodysuit-like costumes, copying the people that came from outer space.

Also, reptilians that could fly seemed to have strong attachment to flying. I am not sure why. Maybe they had a memory of traveling through space. There were quite a lot of them, but gradually some began to feel less need to fly. Those that didn't feel this way branched off into a bird species. In fact, benefits of flying had decreased and having front legs had become more beneficial than having wings. So, those that developed four legs gradually became dominant.

4
The Living Environment in the Age of Elohim

INTERVIEWER

Back then, how were the people who came from outer space living on earth? Also, how advanced was Earth's technology at that time?

ELOHIM

This was a difficult issue. Those who came from outer space all had advanced scientific technology, but it did not mean they could stay long on Earth and live there. For most beings from other planets, the environment of Earth was not suitable. Many could not live without creating a special environment. For example, even if they built a building on Earth, they could not live in it unless they created an environment similar to the inside of their spaceships. In a sense, the environment of Earth itself was quite toxic for space people to live as they were.

In times even before I was on earth, poisonous gases were emitted everywhere from the ground surface because volcanoes were much more active than today. Sulfuric gas and other gases emitted from volcanoes were in many cases toxic, so it was hard for them to live as they were in that environment.

In most cases, they had to wear some kind of protective clothing and when they had to work on earth, grey-type aliens were often used. Greys are very similar to each other in features and appearances. Those were robots or cyborgs that worked on behalf of space people. Many used such cyborgs to carry out activities on earth. It was not easy for them to consider this planet as their permanent residence. A lot of effort was required.

They constructed habitable buildings that, for example, weakened Earth's gravity. Also, the water itself was toxic to the space people; they would sometimes die or develop a sore from drinking it, or they would suffer burns if the water were poured on them. Especially, the earlier the era, the more acidic the water on Earth was, so the environment was quite challenging for them. To make the equivalent of drinking water, they needed to make Earth's water similar to what had existed on their own planet, and not all food on Earth was appropriate for them, either. So, they conducted many kinds of research.

In such circumstances, it was difficult for people with different ways of thinking and lifestyles to coexist. Therefore, some racial struggle or ethnic conflict as it is called now also existed in the past.

INTERVIEWER
Please teach us what the city you lived in and your palace looked like.

ELOHIM
There were differences, more or less, but where I lived was made of pretty sturdy material. People today might not believe it, but we used material that was similar to glass. Quartz was abundant, so we processed the quartz to make something similar to glass that was relatively sturdy.

The houses were not shaped like the ones you see today. Half-circled, dome-typed houses were popular, but some people liked pyramid-shaped ones, as you (the interviewer) also do. They were very good as protection against many things.

Regarding the size, the dome-shaped ones were about 20 meters (about 66 feet) in diameter. I believe one family could live in each one. The pyramid-shaped ones, in many cases, signified status and so there were bigger ones. The ones with a height of about 50-100 meters (about 164-328 feet) had already existed in my time. These were pyramid-shaped, palace-styled dwellings made of quartz and they were apparently made to protect people from fierce dinosaur-like creatures. People constructed buildings that such creatures could not destroy.

INTERVIEWER

What was your palace like? It seems Lord Alpha had lived in a pyramid that floated in the air.

ELOHIM

That must have been a very convenient age. Ours weren't floating in the air, but some of ours had a basement. This was because sometimes there were attacks from outer space, and unlike dinosaurs, these were hard to avoid. Our houses could possibly be destroyed. So, we had built basement areas as a shelter that would not be destroyed by attacks from outer space. During our age, there were air raid warnings because sometimes, space people would come and attack unexpectedly. Earth was "crowded" with various space people.

After all, until they reached a consensus on what sort of races, species, or humankind they aimed to be, we couldn't clearly distinguish which beings were and were not suited to Earth. We were letting them live freely as a civilization experiment, but gradually, we had to tell some of them, "Sorry, you cannot live here," meaning, "It's physically impossible" or "You wouldn't be able to coexist physically." Nevertheless, many of them still wanted to live on Earth. So, when things did not work out, sometimes we had them live far away.

Regarding food, there was an increasing number of animals on land and fish-like creatures underwater, so there wasn't much trouble in securing food. Also, there had already been some level of agriculture, and experiments were carried out on what types of crops would adapt to Earth. So, it's right to assume there were already prototypes of grain-like crops.

INTERVIEWER
Please tell us about the shape of your palace.

ELOHIM

Mine was a bit different from other people's houses. The center was pyramid-shaped, and there were tent-shaped structures, like I mentioned, surrounding it for protection.

5
Elohim's Power

INTERVIEWER

Please tell us about how you looked normally and during battle. We learned in a space people reading that you grew giant and opened the eye on your forehead when you fought.

ELOHIM

The more people hear things like that, the more they're going to think I'm a monster, which I don't want, so I must be careful how I phrase things [*laughs*]. But physically, I was definitely bigger than people today. Normally, I was about three meters (about 10 feet) tall. That was me in my usual form.

You mentioned the third eye. It's true that, in addition to the two human eyes, I had a third eye on my forehead. It's usually closed, but during emergencies or battles, I would open my third eye. It's a psychic eye. In modern terms, it's like a sensor. With it, I could sense others' movements even in the dark, and it could emit a kind of ultrasonic wave. I could measure the distance to an enemy, for example. In other words, it functioned like radar. Not only could I see the enemies physically, but I could also see them in my mind as if using sonar. When enemies approached, I could tell their number and their distance using my third eye. It would begin to function during emergencies like that.

Also, at first glance, I usually looked like a human, but if you looked closely, you would see that I actually had foldable wings stored between my shoulders and back. When necessary, I could spread these out into magnificent archangel-like wings. When I wanted to fly, I could. It was very inconvenient to have huge wings spread out all the time when living on the ground, so usually, I kept them folded and stored. But they would rise up and spread out when I wanted to, so I could fly.

As for whether or not I grew giant... My explanation might be hard to understand. I'm not sure if modern people will understand. In terms of technology, I guess you could say I transformed. I had the ability to do that from the beginning. Well, I don't know if you can say that I actually got bigger, but I had a device on my belt that made me appear bigger, at least. It made me look like I had grown huge to other people. I am not saying it was my true form, but when I touched the center of my belt, the device made me look huge to animals, humans, and other creatures. So, when dinosaurs or evil space people showed up, I could make myself look like a giant. I was usually about three meters tall, but when I used this device to appear huge, I could make myself look twenty meters tall.

INTERVIEWER
How did you fight using your third eye?

ELOHIM
Even now, everyone possesses such a psychic power, right? They all have it, more or less. I just had a stronger version of that. How should I put it? Whether you are an animal or an alien, you naturally have a mind-controlling power or an ability to control the minds of others. It's like the Force. Of course, I had the ability to control others mentally and physically.

Even now, there are plenty of people who have that sort of power. The third eye physically degenerated, but its spiritual function remains. Power is usually emitted from between the eyebrows. If you are strong enough, you can even emit a destructive force. In addition to that, you can manipulate people's minds and make them imagine things, delude them, or fill them with fear.

I don't know if I should call it a beam. I'm not sure if people could see it, but I think it was something like that. Large statutes of Buddha have a dot, also called the Urna, between their eyebrows, right? The dot on the forehead is a trace of the third eye.

I definitely had something along those lines. From my forehead, I mainly emitted the power to control people's minds. I could also use some telekinesis. Using powerful shock waves, I could send objects flying away from me, destroy them, lift them up, or drop them. Against bird-like creatures or pterosaurs, I could emit a type of ultrasonic wave from my third eye. When I stared at it and concentrated on making it fall, I could make it suddenly fall out of the sky. Not everyone had this power. Although some people had similar powers, mine were much more powerful.

6
The Truth of the Space War on Earth

INTERVIEWER

We heard there was a war with invaders from space. Please tell us about it.

ELOHIM

The first group of reptilians were invited from the Magellanic Clouds. They were a comparatively mild race for reptilians. But there were also the second and third groups from the Magellanic Clouds that had caused the first group to flee to Earth. These groups headed for Earth in droves to chase those who had escaped. Those who had already been living on Earth were aware of the need to defend Earth. So, they needed to devise a way to drive away such violent space people and stop them from ruling Earth. This was one reason.

Another reason was the space people from Centaurus. In addition to the space people from the Magellanic Clouds, two different races came from Centaurus—the Alpha Centaurians, who were relatively warm-hearted, and the Beta Centaurians, who were scientifically highly advanced but cold-hearted, typical of some scientists. The latter were reasonable but somewhat lacking in love. We accepted the Alpha Centaurians and then, the Beta Centaurians came. They were extremely advanced in scientific technology, but from the perspective of Earth's values, they were heartless; they slaughtered the weak, one after the other, without hesitation. We were troubled not only by (the latter groups of) reptilians (from the Magellanic Clouds) who were apt to see humans as their food and were extremely barbarous, but also by this race of Centaurians who had an excessive interest in destructive power or destruction. So, we had to fight both groups (the latter groups of reptilians from the Magellanic Clouds and the Beta Centaurians).

It was quite a fierce battle. Especially, the Beta Centaurians had weapons equivalent to today's nuclear weapons. So, it was hard to guide them to change their minds. Of course, they were capable of traveling through space at a velocity faster than the speed of light, so they had already possessed the level of nuclear technology earthlings have now, long, long ago. The current earthlings cannot even send their rockets at the speed of light. The Centaurians, in a sense, had scientific weapons that were capable of destroying a small planet. They could have obliterated the whole planet if earthlings didn't obey them. They had a clear intention of colonizing Earth.

Those who came later from the Magellanic Clouds, and in particular, those from Planet Zeta were apt to raise humans as food and other suitable mammalians as livestock. On the other hand, to put it bluntly, the Beta Centaurians saw battle as a game; they found joy in defeating others. I'm sure there are still many people like this even today. Winning—most sports are about winning against the opponent, right? There is the way of thinking which says that it is good to have winner and losers. This joy of winning over someone is a trace of their tendency. Briefly put, the Beta Centaurians loved war. To be precise, they loved using science and technology to destroy their opponents, so they had a variety of weapons.

Of course, they also had nuclear weapons, which they didn't use right away. They had a bunch of weapons to be used before nuclear weapons. Their weapons were different from modern ones. They sent something down, so they could engage in a proxy war with the people on earth all while they stayed on board their spaceships. Sometimes, they would control various kinds of rockets and missiles from their spaceships as if they were playing a game. At other times, they would send robots with a unique appearance down to the surface to destroy things. These combat robots looked very much like the Earth-invading space people. In this way, they sent such things to the Earth's surface and had them fight without being engaged in direct combat.

There were such space people who loved destroying others as if they were playing games. Those who had assimilated into earthlings and lived a long time on Earth appeared a little weak against such belligerent space people, so they needed to get help from other space people.

These sorts of proxy space wars were also going on during my time. So, there were certainly wars between the space people trying to protect Earth and the ones trying to destroy or invade it.

INTERVIEWER
Please tell us what kinds of weapons humans used at the time.

ELOHIM

Civilizations of each planet were a little different in their level of development. Some of them were destroyed while others survived. So, it is safe to say that the survivors had enough power.

In fact, in order to win, we had to have them come down to the surface. If they came down to the surface, we had the advantage because we were better at moving on the surface. They weren't used to the gravity, air, and other sensations of the ground, so mainly, we attacked their weak points that came from these factors. Once they got used to them, it would be very difficult for us to win.

For the ground battle, we had fighting vehicles somewhat similar to what are now called tanks. They were shaped a bit differently, but we did have tank-like vehicles that were capable of shooting shells. These vehicles did not have caterpillar tread but instead, proper wheels. They also had a turret from which something like cannonballs were fired. So, we had weapons that were capable of destroying, to some point, the space people who came down to the surface to attack us.

If a target were too high up in the air, it would be beyond the range of our tanks, but for flyers, we had weapons that were somewhat like anti-aircraft guns. We were able to shoot down things that were up to a certain altitude. We also had glider-like devices that could be attached to the body. Some people would put these on and fight with weapons while flying through the air. We also had explosives, so we attacked our enemies using explosives in the air. It might sound a little strange, but it was something like this:

People put glider-like devices on their body. Races that had wings could fly on their own, whereas others would wear gliders and carry something similar to a bow. And while flying, they would fire arrows tipped with small, cone-shaped explosives. We had weapons that would explode when they hit an enemy.

Also, for enemies who came down to earth in physical bodies, we had weapons that were effective against their bodies. We could make full use of penetrating weapons, like knives, spears, and bows. They were shaped a bit differently than they are today, but we had the kinds of things that humans can come up with. As for blades, ours were not made of steel like the ones used today. But we had some very hard minerals and we already had the technology to process them, so we used them to make these weapons.

Those who were leading more primitive lives than us weren't able to create advanced weapons. But there were materials that, if heated and pounded, would crack into thin pieces like mica. Some of them had razor-sharp edges, so if these were used as arrowheads or spearheads, they would be sharp enough to kill animals and space people with physical bodies. Some people made such weapons, while others like us used weapons made from something like metals.

Space wars were a reality. Also, space defense forces had been organized to defend Earth mainly by the planets in Vega and they were always on patrol. At times of crisis, people from other planets would rush to aid and defend Earth. So, I think there was a well-formed alliance.

INTERVIEWER
Please tell us what intentions these various groups of space people had for coming to Earth.

ELOHIM
I think it had something to do with our roots before being born on Earth, in other words, our roots before we came to Earth to build a new civilization. Earth's main power or thinking, namely Earth's wisdom and justice, came from

humanoid space people who used to live in Vega and Pleiades. They held quite a lot of those ideas.

Pleiadians valued beauty, harmony, and prosperity to some extent, while Vegans focused on transformation. So, the Pleiades were a civilization based on ego. In the Pleiades, people aimed to make progress by refining their ego as much as possible and beautifying themselves, whereas Vega was a world of infinite egolessness. The basic Vegan approach was to create utopia by doing their best to eliminate their ego and create harmony with those around them.

Pleiadians and Vegans headed in different directions. They were trying to create a utopian society in different ways. The Pleiades had a slightly more advanced civilization. From the viewpoint of the warlike races I just mentioned, Pleiadians had a somewhat happy-go-lucky attitude. So, they were often targeted by aggressive races. Over a long period, they were gradually driven into a corner and many of them fled to other planets, mainly to the Vegan system. Some civilizations in the Pleiades were wiped out. Those who came to Vega from Pleiades thought that the ideology of selflessness alone was not enough for Vega and they suggested adopting other concepts like beauty and grace. In this way, they brought a little more balance or a change to the Vegan value system.

So, the main group of civilization came to Earth via the Pleiades and Vega, and they generally formed the central values of Earth. Other space people were also here, so the fundamental issue was to figure out how to assimilate them.

In a sense, both the Pleiadian and Vegan civilizations had originally come from the Venusian civilization. One civilization sought a way to become divine through an extreme focus on the self and aimed at such type of human development. The other sought to achieve divinity in great harmony through an extreme focus on selflessness. And these civilizations gradually began to merge together. Both elements were introduced to Earth.

However, because these elements were not enough to bring about sufficient progress, some reptilians were also introduced, though they tended to be a bit competitive. This caused a slight change in civilization, but it also gave rise to conflicts. Differences in their thinking and behavioral patterns sometimes led to conflict between people living on Earth. At the same time, others from or related to their home planet also started to come to Earth.

The Descent of Elohim: Spiritual Messages for the Movie,
The Laws of the Universe - The Age of Elohim

So, it became very much like *Star Wars*. There had been space wars on other planets even before various space people arrived on Earth. Such wars have been fought over and over again. A planet in the Pleiades was once destroyed and maybe another in Cygnus. Several other planets might also have been destroyed.

So, I can say that alliances were formed in the process and while some groups could help each other, others could not.

INTERVIEWER
How did other planets cooperate in defending Earth?

ELOHIM
There were several different types of space people, and among them were those that were even more ferocious than the so-called fierce reptilians. So, one issue was how to restrain them. Another issue was how to restrain the group of reptilians that fought using science and technology as though they were playing a game. They seemed to be playing a murder game like in the movie, *The Hunger Games*. These were the two basic types of

reptilians we were up against. And it was an extremely difficult challenge to create a world where many different people prosper in harmony with others. That's why we needed those who could lead them. Each space people, for example Vegans, had their own defenders and leaders, but they were not enough. So, there came volunteer armies who dared to go to other planets and protect those who had immigrated from the Pleiades and Vega. I must say there were heroes in these *Star Wars*-style battles.

One group was related to Vega. Another was a volunteer army from the Andromeda Galaxy that came to help us to suppress extremely scientifically advanced races and extremely ferocious races. The third was a group from Sagittarius led by Jesus Christ. They tried to weaken ferocious reptilians philosophically through the teachings of love and sacrifice, and by emitting extremely powerful feelings of love. They opposed war and slaughter, and they opposed a prey-predator relationship among all living beings. They were led by Jesus Christ and among them were the now well-known angels. Most of them tried not to engage in actual battles. They were the third group that would fight by bringing cultural changes. These three volunteer armies were in charge of defending Earth.

7
Asking about the Evil God of the Universe

INTERVIEWER

Please tell us about the relationship between the evil god of the universe and the space people who came to invade Earth.

ELOHIM

It's complicated. There is what is considered evil and the source of it in the universe or from the perspective of the Earth spirit group. Something like the Idea of Evil surely exists. You could think of it as a destructive function in the universe.

You cannot discard it completely. Stars, planets, and civilizations will eventually come to an end. Trees and leaves eventually decompose, but this is part of the metabolic process. Animals die, but it is important for their carcasses to decompose back into the soil. There are bacteria that cause decomposition. Such "destructive process" is necessary for the metabolic process of the universe as a whole or the reincarnation of planets. Those who are undertaking the role of destruction can be naturally viewed as evil if you look at them within a set time frame.

For example, humans consider illness to be evil. It would be better if it didn't exist, right? Illness is evil, so is an accident. Murder is also evil. But these things happen. Those things are evil, but you cannot live in this world forever, so your life comes to an end when things like illnesses, accidents, murders, or suicides occur. You cannot escape death.

That is why life in this three-dimensional universe is created and destroyed. Creatures are born and then they pass away. On a larger scale, ethnicities and races are created and destroyed. Celestial bodies themselves are also created and destroyed. Living beings in this three-dimensional universe may not like this, but such function does exist. The so-called dark side of the universe is at the root of this function, and it makes this universe a dualistic world of good and evil.

There are beings pulling the strings behind the scenes. But from their point of view, this is one of the reasons why the universe exists. In other words, love is not everything. It's sad when your loved one dies, but their death gives rise to something new. It's sad to lose your parents, but by losing them, you become a parent and raise your children. It's sad when a civilization falls, but a new civilization will rise somewhere else. I believe this is why such function is allowed to work to some extent. In a sense, these beings play the role of "bad guys" in the universe. There is such an aspect to them. You can assume that they appear in areas where they can easily affect people and work on them.

8
The Meaning of Earth in the Universe

INTERVIEWER

So, space people have been fighting over Earth. Does this mean it's a special planet in the universe?

ELOHIM

It's not like that. Many similar situations can be found throughout the universe. In a sense, the universe itself is governed by "local governments." We're only talking about Earth because we are living on it right now. In other galaxies, many other stories are playing out. Similar battles are being fought.

For example, a planet in the Pleiades was ultimately defeated in such a battle. In those times, the people there would value their ethnic purity. They had a strong tendency not to accept anything that differed from them. And because of that, they didn't think of adapting ways other than theirs, even though they had to fight against those that were different from them. It means they had a single culture. People who grew up only in the culture of beauty are weak. Beautiful beings are generally weak. Ugly beings are stronger, to put it bluntly. Pleiadians couldn't do ugly things, so they weren't very good at fighting. And that led to the destruction of their civilization.

To use the example of a familiar space people, once Pleiadians gained experience, they gained wisdom. Then, they changed the way they thought. Vega is another example. Vegans haven't been winning all the time. One of Vega's companion stars was invaded. They experienced that, so they gradually gained wisdom. It's easier to form teams with others that we are spiritually connected with.

Looking at the whole universe, many other civilizations are developing. Earth just happens to be in its best time right now. Its time has come. Life forms were created and civilizations were born, and now is the time for Earth to make further development. That's why it's being used like that. But there are many other planets like Earth and different kinds of people are doing something similar. Galaxies are huge. The universe itself is huge. There exist countless other galaxies similar to the one that you belong to. And you are active only within the scope of what you are aware of.

9
What Did Jesus' Soul Bring to the Earth Civilization?

INTERVIEWER
Please tell us what sorts of ideas and values were brought by the space soul of Jesus when he came to aid Earth.

ELOHIM
Edgar Cayce recommended twice that you conduct a space people reading of Jesus Christ, but this recording came first, so it hasn't happened yet. The content of a space people reading of Jesus would be quite unbelievable to Christians. It would make them tremble. But from your point of view, it's almost time for that. You need to ask him why he is here (on Earth). I think you should ask him directly at some other time.

From our point of view, Abraham was... People who believe in God tend to think that sacrifice is proof of faith, or faith comes with sacrifice, right? It comes from Jewish thought. They think that sacrifice, or in other words, suffering persecution, calamities, and the wrath of God, are all for the sake of faith; they think faith is accompanied by sacrifice. Fundamentally, they believe that offering such sacrifices is the greatest way to show their love for God. You will have to ask Jesus, but it seems he brought in this way of thinking as part of the Earth civilization.

He has kindness at his base. But you should be careful with kindness. People can be kind because they are strong, but at the same time, those who are kind can be weak. In short, they (Jesus and the people who he brought with him) were kind but a little weak, and apt to fall victim to others. It means they believe that their lives in this world are not so important, and that they can increase their faith by thinking little of their lives. Jesus' crucifixion proves he is a savior and Christians see it as a way of saving people. But if you think about it, the idea that says "humans are saved by crucifying the one who came to save them" contains an extremely abnormal thinking. Even so, it is true that his idea (of saving the weak) exists on Earth. It's one of the ideas that are currently dividing Earth. Left-wing liberalism in Japan and the views held by the Democratic Party in the U.S. have such tendency;

they are apt to side with minorities, people suffering from discrimination, and heretics, and crush the strong. This trend is part of the Light of Justice.

10
The Protector of Elohim

INTERVIEWER

In the time of Alpha, there was Gaia. What role did she have and what did she look like during your time?

ELOHIM

Do you want me to tell you that? Well, there was someone to protect me, of course. Gaia considered herself a protector. She defended Earth, but her mission was... She defended Earth, of course, but there were many other people who fought for Earth, so she mainly... I think Gaia's main mission was to protect me.

As for what she looked like, she had to be both a mother and a warrior for defense. Actually, under the cooperation with (the bear-type space people from) the Andromeda Galaxy, she had her body modified by crossing her genes with those of the most powerful being in the Andromeda Galaxy. So, she wasn't just a bear. She was a bear with an appearance that represented both good and evil. The prototype of the giant panda was created in this way, using genes from the Andromeda Galaxy.

She was no ordinary panda. Usually, she had the embracing, "furry" love of a mother, but in an emergency, she would extend her claws as powerful weapons. She was like one of the X-Men that was mentioned earlier. Who's the most powerful member of the X-Men? Wolverine, right? Her claws were the giant panda's kung fu fist. Simply put, she would extend her strong iron-like claws and use them to knock down her enemies using kung fu. When necessary, she would even extend the claws on her feet. She would have four weapons with a total of twenty claws and use them freely to shred through her enemies. It was mainly a defensive kind of kung fu. She would transform into this frightening giant panda and the look in her eyes would naturally change as well; they would shine like burning flames. In the worst case, meaning when she was the angriest, even a horn would come out of her panda head as her final weapon. It was a big horn, like a unicorn's. She would grow a horn and use it to headbutt her enemies. She would charge in with huge claws and a huge horn on her head. That was her basic fighting style.

That was enough because she was dedicated to defense. She heavily guarded the area around me and focused on beating up anyone who tried to sneak up on me. Usually, she looked like a kind, generous, and affectionate mother, but at times, she provided that sort of powerful defense. She never went on expeditions to attack enemies. Mainly, she dedicated herself to defending the area around my palace.

Her body was made from genetic mutation, and her body became the prototype to be imitated later on. You could consider the form of the modern panda—the messenger of love and peace—to be a partial remnant of her image.

INTERVIEWER
What was Gaia's name during your time?

ELOHIM
Huh? Umm... Pan... Pan... Pan... Uhh... Panguru. You can call her Panguru.

11
The Teachings of Elohim

INTERVIEWER

Please tell us what sorts of teachings you preached at the time.

ELOHIM

I mainly taught the basic teachings of religion, I mean, the teachings of good and evil, while taking into consideration the times and the environment. The forces of darkness or the powers of the dark world were attacking us, so I focused on teaching about Light, faith, and good and evil.

The teachings of Jesus might have been partially included in my teachings. I firmly impressed upon people, using various means, the following: "It's not good to just invade and slaughter others. All living things want to live a long life and prosper. You should understand this and establish justice to maintain harmony and order. Then, you should teach people about good and evil, and focus on avoiding evil and promoting good."

Fighting evil can sometimes give birth to another evil, but fighting in self-defense was acceptable. This was my thinking. It is not very desirable for the righteous to be completely destroyed, nor is it good for the wicked to flourish. It is better for the righteous to develop and prosper. This was how I thought.

I'm very sorry that this session was about "a world of monsters."

INTERVIEWER

Thank you very much for sharing such a precious, long story with us today.

ELOHIM

If you need anything else, ask me again. I don't know if this information should be revealed so easily. Some of it probably should be kept secret.

Thank you.

RYUHO OKAWA

[*Claps twice.*] It was a mythical age. But I think He described it in a way that's easier for us to imagine. I think we need to read between the lines to make a story out of this, though.

Anyway, He spoke to us, so we should be able to make a good movie if we visualize it and add more touches to the story to improve it. For now, please use this as the firsthand material.

Thank you very much.

CHAPTER TWO

A Spiritual Message from Elohim
—Elohim and His Age—

Originally recorded in Japanese on February 13, 2018
at the Special Lecture Hall of Happy Science in Japan
and later translated into English.

The interviewers are referred to as A and B.

The background of the recorded spiritual message

To supplement the script for the movie, *The Laws of the Universe - The Age of Elohim*, we asked Lord Elohim about the time when He was alive on earth.

1
The Age of Elohim and What Happened After That

The risk for the souls to be born in a physical body

ELOHIM

What else do you need to know?

A

At this stage, we have decided on the characters, but we almost have nothing but battles in the story. So, leaving aside the characters for now, could you tell us what it was like in your time?

ELOHIM

Hmm. The earthly world was primitive, so it was very dangerous for the souls to be born. Because many physical bodies were very primitive, it was highly likely that the souls would degrade spiritually by living in physical bodies. Souls that wouldn't have degraded if they stayed in the spirit world were very likely to deteriorate spiritually by being born into this world. They were fighting like savages, so they would inevitably regress. That was my impression.

But in this world, you can experience what you can't in the spirit world. How can I explain the spirit world? When you watch a movie, for example, you do not assume the actions of the main characters are actually happening, right? But spirits in the spirit world assume the image in front of them is actually happening there. In the earthly world, you feel hurt when you are hit. But even if spirits believe they are hitting each other in the spirit world, it may not be actually happening because it is their imagination.

Seen from the other world (spirit world), this world, or the three-dimensional world, is fictional, but as you live in the three-dimensional world, you will gradually feel that the spirit world is fictional. People started to develop reversed values in this way. That was my time. So, I had to teach people not to lose sight of their true nature as spiritual beings. I would teach them, "If you prefer living in this world, or if your major concern or main purpose of life is set on satisfying your desire for power, status, or wealth, or your lust for the opposite sex, you will have no place to return to after death." That was how it was in my age.

When a large number of people, I mean, hundreds of millions of people are sent down into this world, they will submit to earthly values. When there is no food, they are desperate to get food. If they are carnivores, blood will be shed. Sometimes lives are lost. If they don't eat meat, they have to constantly do taxing work such as farming.

Basically, people were more likely to increase their level of civilization when they were agricultural. Of course, even if they fed on animals, they had to make weapons and traps to catch them.

So, you are strongly bound to the earthly life if you have to eat to survive. Under these circumstances, it is very difficult to teach people that the true world is the other world that cannot be seen. I think it was during our time that for the very first time, people were taught faith in the true sense. I taught, "Believe in the world you cannot see."

A

Let me ask you from another perspective. What kind of movie do you *not* want us to depict?

ELOHIM

Well... I guess you want to make it something like *Star Wars*, but that is only the fruit of poor imagination of modern people. It just looks like only machines have evolved. And most of the spiritual elements and faith are depicted as the Force. It's one kind of psychic power... It's almost like a faith in psychic power. In this sense, there's no depth to it at all.

A

There is no depth in its spirituality.

ELOHIM

In our time, it was very risky for the higher spirits to come down to the earth. We were born from the higher realms of the spirit world and had to live under the same condition as others—residing in a normal physical body and eating food to survive. At the same time, we had to encourage people to have faith in the world of God and the world of high spirits, and create the conditions for them to return there, all the while we were alive on earth. It was a very, very difficult thing to do. It is very difficult to make people believe in something invisible.

Everyone essentially has spiritual abilities, but as people chased their prey and engaged in tribal wars in this world, they gradually lost a lot of these abilities. This is the truth.

It is true that space people had come to Earth and a lot of them became ancestors of human species and other animals. So, human beings did not evolve simply by natural selection as Darwin said. They have certainly evolved, but they may have more regressed than evolved. Earth had been regressing to a large extent. So, to stop that regression, I had to teach people faith in God, as a "jet propulsion" against corruption.

The beginning of hell

A

Earlier, when you were talking about the movie, *The Laws of the Universe - Part III*, you mentioned that the recent World War I and World War II had an aspect of the fight against materialism and communism.

ELOHIM

Materialism basically means, "There is this world only," right? Since there is only this earthly world that you live in, all that matters is how you strategically enlarge your territory and become the ruler of this world, right? But it's not true. It's fundamentally wrong.

However, people living on earth can see this world only, so many people agree with that idea. In reality, the bigger the field, the better; the bigger the rice paddy, the better; and the more fish you can get, the better. So, you would naturally give in to the desire to get as much share as possible. That's why it was very important to fight against the causes that led to corruption.

A

Were you born on earth because such evil or evil way of thinking began to form in an obvious manner?

ELOHIM

It's not like that. Actually, there naturally arose differences in people's earthly conditions such as food, house, or social class. There were also differences between men and women, or in what people wore. What used to be a means to live in this world gradually became an end, and people became obsessed with acquiring such things. But eventually, people have to leave this world. After they die, they have to return to the other world. When those people returned to the other world, they could no longer live in the heavenly world of light where they had originally come from.

What did they do when they couldn't return to the heavenly world? Naturally, they had to find a place to live in the area near the earthly world. Just like a mole digging in the ground to find a place to live, they started to build their home closer to the ground surface. So, they became "subterranean" in the other world. They started to build their home underground and tried to create a place where they wouldn't have to look at the heavenly world, or a place where they could be free from the hawk eyes of the heavenly world.

Obviously, people who didn't believe in God, Buddha, or high spirits while they were alive in this world can't return to heaven straightaway after they die. Those who lived a primitive life in this world could only live in the extension of that kind of life. So, they had to wander around on earth, or after a while, they had to create their home on their own. That is how the lower spirit world began to form.

It is said that heaven was created starting from the top, with the last realm being the Astral Realm located between heaven and this world, where souls are born from and return to. It is also a place where souls gather after they die. Even so, it was inhabited by those who had lived rightly in the spiritual sense.

But among the souls who returned from the earthly world, there were some who could not go up because their spiritual weight was too heavy. In time, those souls created places like the shade of a rock, caverns, underground space, or caves, and began to live there. This was actually the beginning of hell. Such places were gradually formed, and the number of souls who live there increased. It is just like moles gathering and building many underground passages in the garden where there are a lot of food, vegetables, and fruits. Those souls could not return to heaven.

The origin of devils and the establishment of hell

ELOHIM

In the battles between human beings, there will naturally be those who fight with the Will of God in mind and those who fight for their own greed by ignoring God's Will and trying to increase their followers. Even though they both fight and die, their destinations are different, of course.

There are times when people kill others, but sometimes they must or should do so to carry out justice, and sometimes they must not do so. There are both cases. The case you are allowed to kill people is when they have formed an evil organization and are repeatedly committing unjustifiable deeds. Those people must take responsibility for their own behavior and be punished in this world. It is too late if they come to understand good and evil only after returning to the other world, so they need to learn to discern good and evil while they are still alive.

That is why judgment is necessary in this world. It means that the leaders need to be strong and that there must be a system to punish those who break the law, code, social contract, or the code of community life. Judgment or punishment manifests in this world by defeating the rebels or executing the leader of the rebels. This was actually the origin of Satan or devils.

Such a situation continued for about 30 million years after my time, and about 120 million years ago, Lucifer became a fallen angel. He is Michael's twin brother and was often referred to as "the Son of Dawn" when he was a trouble to the divine realm of the spirit world. He was known as the Son of Dawn, and he was indeed a shining angel in appearance. But when he was born on earth, he went astray; he was driven by strong greed and, simply put, became like the First Emperor of the Qin Dynasty. He started to crave for eternal life on earth.

He could hear God's voice at first, but he gradually denied it. He said to God, "You and I think differently," or "My thinking is different from yours." He would say, "You may be my Father, but you're nothing more than that. You cannot be omniscient and omnipotent, and I don't think you have the authority to make all the rules for things in this world. You should leave earthly matters to the people on earth. It's up to the people on earth to come up with the rules and practice what they think is fair and equal. Those who don't live on earth have no right to interfere. It's OK for those who listen to God to occasionally come out as messiahs or prophets and propagate God, but they should not have actual power on earth." He meant, "The strongest people should hold power on earth and the person who controls the most people is the greatest on earth. The one who controls a greater number of people and makes them obey is great." That's what Lucifer started to preach.

It is said that what caused Lucifer to rebel against God was his jealousy toward God. In fact, he wanted to become omniscient and omnipotent. Just as God creates the rules and the laws of the universe, he, too, wanted to make his own kingdom by making everyone follow what he said and what he thought. He wanted to make this world his kingdom. That is his starting point.

However, even if he wanted to make this world his kingdom, there are "birth, aging, illness, and death" to the life on earth. When people grow old, they will eventually leave this world. At that time, those who did not obey the voice of God and instead turned their back on Him by saying, "I think differently from you," will be ashamed to face God. So, Lucifer had no choice but to join those who were in the shadows. But because he had a strong spiritual power, he went on to dig even deeper into hell. As a result, the underground world gradually expanded and hell was firmly established during Lucifer's time.

The two ways to clean out hellish values

A
So, the spiritual training in this world is severe and even a soul that was once a god or a light of angel can become like him (a fallen angel or devil). Is that what you mean?

ELOHIM
Actually, wearing a physical body often makes you spiritually blind. If you are wearing the Lovely Panda costume when you sing and dance to "Panda-Roonda"...

A
Ah, yes, it's heavy.

ELOHIM

You probably can't see the world. It's the same thing. You are in such a condition. You can no longer see the truth (once you are in a physical body).

When humans first lived in this world, many of them had a pure mind, so they were able to hear the voices from the heavenly world, they knew the existence of the heavenly world, and they were able to receive inspiration from their guardian spirits, all while they were alive. But gradually, they lost the ability to receive the opinions of their guardian spirits, and various ghosts, evil ghosts, and devils wandering on earth began to lure people. And, some people followed their voices. These spirits would whisper things like, "You will be at an advantage if you take the small neighboring country" or "You deserve the larger share." As a result, quarrels between siblings would also occur. There would be fights over inheritance or women. Brothers might fight over a beautiful woman. Conflicts would occur between parents and children, as well. So, it's tough. It's really tough.

In this way, hellish values were established after my time. I had been concerned about that even after I returned to the heavenly world, but it happened. So, we thought about how to clean out these values. One way was to start this world from scratch again. We could destroy all living things in this world by natural disasters such as earthquakes, tsunamis, sinking, volcanic eruptions, meteorites hitting Earth, or other environmental changes, and start all over again. This was one way. Another way was to send down spirits who have different views, that is, saviors or prophets, to this world and have them preach to people. However, gradually these saviors or prophets... There weren't always many people who openheartedly believed and followed them. Fake saviors and prophets also appeared. Sometimes, devils pretended to be saviors or prophets. But living people couldn't tell the difference, so they sometimes ended up believing them. That is why this world has been getting closer to the devil's world than to God's world. This is the story of a fallen angel.

2
The Formation of Hell and the Dark Side of the Universe

What human beings are tested to see

B

We will be portraying this in Part II of *The Laws of the Universe*, but was there any involvement by aliens? I've heard that there was a nuclear war caused by the intervention of aliens.

ELOHIM

Many planets have already been destroyed because of such an event. So, it's true there was a much more powerful weapon than the nuclear weapons that exist in this world now. There were many cases where an entire planet was destroyed. When people are reasonable and there is God's justice, the balance is maintained, but when this balance is lost, such things can happen. For example, when a powerful weapon falls into the hands of evil rulers... well, it's possible that an entire planet is destroyed.

In terms of the current international affairs, if some countries support North Korea to increase their production of nuclear missiles, various ethnic groups will probably be destroyed. But it is difficult for people to tell whether something is good or evil right away.

B
Yes.

A
If I may ask, is there any important point that you would like us to portray in the movie?

ELOHIM
Hmm.

A
I don't think we can necessarily fight out through physical combat or using force alone.

B
Now, the movie story is set on the battle between "Lord Elohim vs. evil aliens & evil gods of the dark side of the universe," but this setting is...

ELOHIM

Hmm. People have different ways of thinking. Even in freedom, there are elements that will lead you to either heaven or hell. Even if you have a certain idea, you don't know what will happen—whether you will succeed or fail—until you actually put it into practice. And even if you succeed, you will also be judged whether your success is confined to this world only or it can be carried over to heaven.

As long as we allow for diversity of thoughts, there will always be the possibility for hell to form. The reason there is hell is... In a society of diverse thoughts, the majority is apt to punish the minority. It always happens. And when that happens, the punished minority will often become lost spirits. This is the reason hell began to form.

But in a democratic society, the opposite can happen—the hellish force can become the majority. In that case, the premise that people have all the power as sovereigns is not necessarily right. There is also the idea that sovereignty lies with God. According to this idea, God might not allow people who don't follow His Will to prosper. In that case, an "angel of destruction" might appear. This is why human beings are continually tested to see if they are aware that they are created beings. On the other hand, it's important for God to maintain His character as the Creator.

When human beings lose qualification as children of God

B
Lucifer was originally named Lucifel, but he fell and became a devil. Was there something from the universe involved in this?

ELOHIM
Umm... It's true that he had come to Earth from another planet. Names with "El" or "el" mean "light of God" mainly in the Middle East including Israel, so I think he was an angel who helped God. But in every age, when a group of people work together, there will always be betrayers or expelled people. At that time, if they are honest and obedient, they can repent, but if they do not

want to reflect on themselves, they will be rejected and isolated from the people around them.

Of course, he was created as a child of God. Even so, or even if he was worshiped as a god, he ended up in hell because he largely went astray from the main road. That's the meaning of his fall. Even if you are a child of God, if you kill a lot of people for an evil purpose using nuclear weapons, for example, then generally speaking, there is a high possibility that you will lose your qualification as a child of God.

A

In your time, there were already many space people that had come from many different planets, weren't there? That's why you appeared and preached the values and justice on Earth. Is that right?

ELOHIM

That's because each planet has different values.

A

Right. They are different.

ELOHIM

There's indeed the idea that justice is on the side of the strong. The weak will be eaten. It's the law of nature. This is definitely true with insects and animals. That's why the weaker animals think of various ways to defend themselves. Some appear in a protective color, while others emit a bad smell, dig holes to hide, or live higher up on trees. They think of protecting themselves in this way. On the other hand, the strong animals think of further evolving by having sharper fangs, longer claws, or faster legs.

In the same way, in the universe as a whole, there is also the idea that the strong should dominate the weak to maintain order. However, if the strong were no more than "just being strong," the wolves could eat up all the sheep, for example. But it is not allowed to go as far as to destroy the balance of nature.

The Descent of Elohim: Spiritual Messages for the Movie,
The Laws of the Universe - The Age of Elohim

The true nature of the souls of Jesus, Michael, and Amaterasu-O-Mikami

A

In your previous spiritual message (Chapter One), you mentioned that space people from Andromeda and Vega, and Jesus also fought on the side of earthlings. Did Jesus have another name at that time?

ELOHIM

Hmm. Well, Jesus is Emmanuel, but before that, he was Amor, of course.

A

Oh, Amor.

ELOHIM

Amor, yes. So, his theme is "love." To explore the nature of love, he carried out various experiments on civilization on earth. As an ethnic god, Amor protected his people. But there was also a side to Amor that went beyond an ethnic god. Also, Amor had a feminine element, which manifested in the attitude of renouncing war or avoiding battle. There were diverse aspects in him, but he basically analyzed the diversity of love.

On the other hand, Michael symbolizes "battle" and "realization of justice." These elements were certainly necessary, but Lucifer was extremely narcissistic. So, "Michael vs. Lucifer" was like a battle between the Sun and the Moon. Michael was the one who gave out light like the Sun, but Lucifer would shine by reflecting the light of the Sun, as the Moon does. So, he wasn't shedding his own light. However, Lucifer developed his false self as he was revered by people. Then, he thought it would be easier for him to aim to be number one in hell, instead of aiming to become like the many angels and high spirits in heaven, or God who they protect.

B
So, he wanted to be number one?

ELOHIM
For instance, if you were born in a giant country like China, you might think, "It's easier to sneak into the CCP

and become its ruler, instead of aiming to be the number one through free competition." It's something like that.

A

Was Amaterasu-O-Mikami there, too, during your time?

ELOHIM

Amaterasu-O-Mikami was... Vegans were a little... Vegans weren't very self-assertive. They tried to survive by blending into others, so they were apt to lose their ground against other space people with strong character. There was such an aspect to them.

B

In times of battle, is it usually the ones who are good at fighting that appear?

A

Was it such people that were fighting?

ELOHIM

When the inhabitants can no longer live on their planet, they intrude into other planets. This occurred many times in the past. Just as countries on Earth have fought each other, there were wars between different planets.

A route connecting hells between planets

A
Not only reptilians, but there were also beings from other planets that came to Earth to settle. Is that right?

ELOHIM
Well, in the beginning, things were lenient on Earth as the place of civilization experiment; all kinds of people were accepted and were allowed to have many possibilities. Gradually, however, there were people who could adapt themselves to the way of Earth and those who couldn't. Among those who could not adapt themselves but were nevertheless attached to Earth, there were some who fell to hell. Some of those who became devils after falling to hell were obviously attached to the idea of turning Earth into a planet like the one they used to live.

The reason why Vegans are strong is because they made efforts to raise their ability to adapt. The ones who have a high degree of adaptability can think, "We should just adapt ourselves to the new environment," but the egotistic ones who wanted to assert themselves and forced their own way without trying to improve their adaptability could not live like Vegans. They didn't want to be humble or adjust themselves to others. There also appeared some who believed themselves to be "God," and they thought, "It's not the way of God."

A
Did you have to harmonize these people?

ELOHIM
Actually, Earth's...

A
What values should...

ELOHIM
I had to decide what love, justice, and Truth were on Earth. When the values of different beings who had come from outer space conflicted with each other, I had to

decide which values to choose or not to choose. I think this eventually became the standard to divide heaven and hell. Of course, I had to accept the diversity of those who had come from other planets, but it did not mean this diversity could be entirely accepted as it was. Whether or not these people could adapt themselves was important.

The life span of human beings is limited. Countless humans have been involved in the formation of hell over tens of millions of years. There were many spirits who fell to hell after dying in battle because they died with chagrin.

Well, there is an argument over whether or not the dark side of the universe exists. Assuming that each planet has a realm where spirits who couldn't return to heaven gather after they die in a war or for some other reasons, it's true that these spirits can connect to each other through the Law of Same Wavelengths. Umm... Well, it's possible that such a back channel has been formed.

B

You mean Kandahar (one of the commanders in charge of invading Earth), right?

ELOHIM

You have a quite imaginative character in your movie (*The Laws of the Universe - Part I*). The leader of a planet that was entirely destroyed might become a demon of vengeance, for example. The leader will then start to gather allies and call for a coalition of hell. So, there are beings that have and govern the route connecting hell of Earth and hell of other planets, although most spirits in hell don't know about that.

The reason light of angels need to be born one after another

A

So, it's not that there is someone like Kandahar who is the root of evil, but there are vengeful thoughts of people whose planets were destroyed after losing in war, and grudges of those who might be called devils. These feelings can be summed up to be an evil character like Kandahar. Is that what you mean?

ELOHIM

There are cases in which space beings come to the new planet to settle but are not allowed to obtain physical bodies there. Unfortunately, although they were once human spirits, they were unable to attain a high level of enlightenment. These spirits are only allowed to live in animal bodies. They are told to start as animals first. In short, this means regression. But it can happen.

There are both meek and aggressive animals. People who have fallen to hell after committing too many murders may be reborn as aggressive animals. People who were killed and held a grudge may be reborn as meek animals. In this way, there are human spirits who reside in the bodies of higher animals. Looking at their appearance, we have to call them as "being regressed."

Over the long history, however, some of those spirits that were born as higher animals have evolved and are now born as humans. Considering the current population growth on Earth, we can assume there are many such spirits who have evolved from animals.

A

I understand. It's like that.

ELOHIM

Things may not go as you expect. It was a time when a hellish world was beginning to form.

A

Hell has evolved further and become what it is now. Is that right?

ELOHIM

Yes, hell itself has become boundless.

A

So, hell has evolved, too.

ELOHIM

But the spirits in hell certainly have their lives, too. It's just like how we can't dig out all the moles that are hiding underground to avoid the sunlight. Earthworms live underground, too. There are such beings. It would be hard to dig them all out and shed light on them.

Hell exists as long as people live in this world. That's the reason why light of angels need to be born into this world one after another to give guidance or guidelines, so that people will not fall to hell.

A
Right.

3
The Danger in "Democracy without God" and "Freedom without God"

A

This is my final question. From your point of view, how do you see what El Cantare is trying to do in this modern age? It might have to do with the sequel, *The Laws of the Universe - Part III*. What do you think about His mission?

ELOHIM

From our viewpoint, the current expansion of democracy contains a lot of abnormal aspects. With "democracy without God," you are entering an age when the people who follow the teachings of God are the minority, because the larger group of people control Earth. This is the biggest problem. People will restrain themselves to some extent if they awaken to faith in God, but the world will dangerously become out of control under "freedom without God." I don't know if human beings will be able to overcome this.

Earth's current population is said to be about 7.6 billion (at the time of the recording), but we think that about 10 billion is the limit. If it goes beyond that, we may somehow need to destroy the ones who are not obedient to God. To do that, disasters such as wars, various kinds of viral diseases, meteorites, earthquakes, tsunamis, volcanic eruptions, and the sinking of continents might befall humans.

You might want to research in more detail the reason why the Mu civilization perished even though it had a great king, and why the Atlantis civilization perished.

A
I see. OK, I understand.

ELOHIM
Why did they have to perish if they were more advanced than the current civilization? There must be some reasons for that.

A
I understand. [*To Interviewer B.*] Do you have anything else?

The Descent of Elohim: Spiritual Messages for the Movie,
The Laws of the Universe – The Age of Elohim

B

No. I'm OK.

A

OK, then...

ELOHIM

OK.

B

Thank you very much.

RYUHO OKAWA

[*Claps twice.*]

A

Thank you very much.

CHAPTER THREE

Lyrics of the Original Songs for the Movie, *The Laws of the Universe - The Age of Elohim*

Originally given in Japanese
and later translated into English.

EDITOR'S NOTE

Master Ryuho Okawa has been creating a lot of lyrics and music, including theme songs and other songs for Happy Science movies. In addition, he has served as the Executive Producer, writing original stories and providing original concepts to the movies. "El Cantare Ryuho Okawa Original Songs," written and composed by Master Okawa, are powerful words of enlightenment and they straightforwardly express the beautiful melodies of the higher dimensions of the heavenly world. Master Okawa's original songs constitute an important part of the original concepts of the movies.

Chapter Three contains the lyrics of the original songs for the movie, *The Laws of the Universe - The Age of Elohim*, which Master Okawa has written and composed prior to the shooting of the movie. They express the core ideas of the movie, the story, and the characters' thoughts and feelings, such as Elohim's boundless mercy toward humanity and the will of Panguru who supports Elohim.

In particular, the song, "The Miracle of You," on page 124 is one of the songs celebrating the marriage of Master Ryuho Okawa and Aide to Master & CEO Shio Okawa. It describes the bond between God Elohim and Panguru. It is also an insert song.

The Descent of Elohim: Spiritual Messages for the Movie,
The Laws of the Universe – The Age of Elohim

"Elohim's Theme"

Words and Music by Ryuho Okawa

Elohim, Elohim, Elohim
Why did you come here again?
Elohim, Elohim, Elohim
What is your new Teachings in this age?

The Earth is a blue and beautiful planet with many animals
There are various ethnic leaders who governed each race and each language
Elohim, you are the one who came here again
To teach them the Supreme Truth of God
All the way you came here, a long, long time ago
Oh yes, definitely you're the Lord of this planet
Elohim, when we call the name of God
When we call the name of the Lord
We know absolutely you would be there in the end
Elohim, O our Lord, our Lord God
Please get rid of all the evil from this planet Earth
Elohim, O our Lord, our Lord God
Beyond the racial differences and colors of the skin

Lyrics of the Original Songs for the Movie,
The Laws of the Universe - The Age of Elohim

To make this planet where people love each other
We need your mercy
Elohim, our only choice is to follow you
So, we believe in you
You are the Father, our Lord

Elohim, you are the origin of love
Elohim, you are the justice itself
Even if Earth is full of sufferings and sadness,
You'll never, never, never forsake us
It's because you are the only Lord
Our Lord God preaches about love and justice
And He will create harmony and peace

Elohim is the name of God
Elohim is the name of the Lord
Elohim, we devote ourselves only to you
Above all ethnic leaders
You are the one, who guided Earth
After the name of Alpha
Elohim, you are the one, who rules this planet Earth
You are the one, who's the source of all teachings

The Descent of Elohim: Spiritual Messages for the Movie,
The Laws of the Universe - The Age of Elohim

Ah Ah, people learn to know God through loving each other
Ah Ah, people learn to know what is goodness itself
Beyond good and evil we will see the justice of God
And we will try to establish lasting peace
We, believers, sincerely wish our dream come true
Elohim, let us spread your name forever
We will do our best

Elohim, please hear our prayers
Elohim, please protect and keep us safe forever
Elohim, I beg you to defeat devils completely
We are children of Light
We want to live in the world, full of Light
Be together with you forever
Thank you very much

The Descent of Elohim: Spiritual Messages for the Movie,
The Laws of the Universe - The Age of Elohim

"Panguru's Theme"

Words and Music by Ryuho Okawa

Ah Ah Ah...
Ah Ah Ah...
Ah Ah Ah...

The time has come
If we don't fight
There is no reason we are here
We must fight to protect Lord Elohim, God of the Earth

Panguru, fight!
Being a woman is no excuse
Fight, Panguru!
Fight, Panguru!
Hiding tears behind your fists
Make a charge, Panguru!
With your heart full of sorrow

I shed tears for peace
Filled with love and courage
I really want to protect you with all my life

Lyrics of the Original Songs for the Movie,
The Laws of the Universe – The Age of Elohim

I really do
It's coming from the bottom of my heart

Being a woman cannot be a weakness
That should never be allowed
To protect the Lord of the Earth
You will fight against any devils
Even demons of the universe

Be strong in our heart and we will fight
Seraphim, hang in there
You will fight with me
We are the last and final fortress to protect our Lord

Holding back my tears
Until I see the peace of the universe
Settle down on the earth
And comfort people

I will blow my tears away
Bring my strength to come alive once again
O Lord, please protect my holy mission

The Descent of Elohim: Spiritual Messages for the Movie,
The Laws of the Universe - The Age of Elohim

"Jesus of the Beginning"

Words and Music by Ryuho Okawa

Uh Uh Uh—

Uh Uh Uh—

Uh Uh Uh Uh—

Uh Uh Uh Uh—

Uh Uh Uh—

From a faraway universe

As I arrived at this planet

It was full of hatred, grief, and rage

I came down into this storm

I fought for the people

To liberate them from the yoke of their sufferings

This is Jesus

Jesus of the Beginning

It's the beginning

People are apt to fall into evil

However, it's not that they intentionally fell into evil

Each one of them tried to improve himself

But in many cases,

His joy turned into the pain and sorrow of others

Lyrics of the Original Songs for the Movie,
The Laws of the Universe – The Age of Elohim

That is why I came to give healing

The defeated ones,

Even if you lose in a fight on the earth

You are not defeated in the true sense

This world is only temporary

You cannot take with you your status, reputation,

Or material wealth to another world

So I came here

To encourage all of you to abandon everything

Abandoning everything will

Lead you to acquire everything

Is it so hard to accept this?

Ah—

That's why I laid down my life for all of you

And sacrificed my life

I showed you the way humans should live

At the cost of my life

What I wanted to teach you is that

To throw your life away is

To help nurture life

And to risk your life

For the sake of someone else

Will nurture yourself

Forgive yourself

And lead you to love yourself for the sake of God

My love is the love of the beginning

This is Jesus of the Beginning

I'm your Savior

The Descent of Elohim: Spiritual Messages for the Movie,
The Laws of the Universe - The Age of Elohim

"Yaizael's Theme"

Words and Music by Ryuho Okawa

Ah Ah Ah —!
Ah Ah Ah —!
Ah Ah Ah —!
Ah Ah Ah —!
O Oh! O Oh! Oh —!
O Oh! O Oh! Oh —!

I'm here, I'm here, I'm here on Earth
What did I come here for?
I surely came to win the fight
Win it! Win it! Win it! Win it!
Yaizael! Win it!
Yaizael! Win it!
You are invincible!
You can beat any space aliens!

You're not scared of dinosaurs on Earth!
You're not scared of demons on Earth!
You're not scared of animals on Earth!

Lyrics of the Original Songs for the Movie,
The Laws of the Universe – The Age of Elohim

You're not scared of human beings!
Go Go! Yaizael!

Go! Go!
Go! Go!
Go! Go!
Go On! Go On!
Go On! Go On! Go On!

Go Go! Go Go! Yaizael!
You are invincible!
Who is the strongest in the universe?
It has got to be Yaizael
You are invincible on the ground
Once you fly up high in the sky
You are invincible also off the ground
Once you spot an enemy from the sky
No one can escape from you
You're gonna roll up all the evil
Smash all the evil at one blow, then establish only justice

The Descent of Elohim: Spiritual Messages for the Movie,
The Laws of the Universe - The Age of Elohim

Go Go! Go Go! Yaizael!
Your time has come!
Who's the guardian deity that protects the Earth
In the world today?
Yaizael! Yaizael! Hey!
Yaizael! Yaizael!
Yaizael is the only one!

If I can win the fight, it will bring us peace
Justice and goodness will become one
God's Will is to choose goodness
Smash all the evil into pieces and promote goodness
Then justice will rise

Go Go! Go Go! Yaizael!
You are invincible on the ground!
You are invincible in the sky!
You are invincible in the universe!
Go Go! Go Go! Yaizael!
No one can defeat you
With your heart in tune with the heart of God
Beat up all the enemies completely

Lyrics of the Original Songs for the Movie,
The Laws of the Universe - The Age of Elohim

Go Go! For the sake of goodness!

Go Go! For the sake of love!

Go Go! For the sake of justice!

Go Go! For the sake of eternal peace!

Yaizael, your name is "Goddess of Victory"

The Descent of Elohim: Spiritual Messages for the Movie,
The Laws of the Universe – The Age of Elohim

"The Miracle of You"

Words and Music by Ryuho Okawa

At the beginning
You were always told off
"So sorry" was the mystical phrase you used
Which became a byword for you

However you were
Never a loser, never ever
Since you came close to me
Miracles started happening to me like a mystery
All of the sudden
I started up a political party
And called for a social reform
I founded two schools
And established a university
Around the globe I traveled on
To teach the Truth in English

I started public spiritual messages
Then even space people appeared

Lyrics of the Original Songs for the Movie,
The Laws of the Universe - The Age of Elohim

When I said to you

"You remind me of a Panda"

I remember

It was on the seashore in Dubai

You gradually

Began to resemble a Panda in your behavior

Suddenly I was rejuvenated

And started curing illnesses of many people

⎛ Ah Elohim! ⎞
⎜ I see it now ⎟
⎝ Your true love is Panguru, the Chanel of ancient times ⎠

(☆ Repeat)

The Descent of Elohim: Spiritual Messages for the Movie,
The Laws of the Universe – The Age of Elohim

"The Fallen Angel's Theme"

Words and Music by Ryuho Okawa

It was a sad story

My twin little brother became jealous of God

And wanted to become God

My name is Michael

The greatest among Seven Archangels

My twin little brother is

The Son of Dawn, Lucifer

He used to be a beautiful young man

But he was blinded by the status and glory of God

And misunderstood God's true will

Hoping that he would be God

He started REVOLUTION

Being his twin soul brother

What I had in my heart was a very, very, very sad feeling

In an effort to try to teach him

There is something more important

Than being a blood relative,

That is being a child of God

I fought with my twin little brother and wielded my sword

Lyrics of the Original Songs for the Movie,
The Laws of the Universe – The Age of Elohim

Faith should always go beyond the family ties

The most important thing in terms of love is faith in God

We must pass on this message

To the generation that follows us

I defeated him with my sword

Shot him down from heaven of the great universe

Struck him to the ground like thunder

Then he fell into hell

The lost human souls that wandered around worshipped him

And set him up as a leader in hell

Ah, since then

120 million years have passed by

During all that time, there has been a constant fight

Between heaven and hell with regard to this earthly world

Even so, my little brother

Who used to be the Son of Dawn, Lucifer

You had your own head cut down by your big brother, Michael

Still you gathered around all the evil spirits in hell

You should know that you will never be able to win

Against God

The Descent of Elohim: Spiritual Messages for the Movie,
The Laws of the Universe – The Age of Elohim

In the world, there are things that can be forgiven

And things that are unforgiven

The Fallen Angel is now called Satan

My twin brother,

Listen to the words of love from your brother

Until you defeat me

God has no intension of laying even one finger on you

Love is stronger than all fears

In this world or even in the other world

There is not a thing that can defeat love

The last day of hell is coming

Until you are born again as the Son of Dawn

Until that day or time comes

My battle will not end

God is watching over people forever

Afterword

Just like the prequel, *The Laws of the Universe - Part I*, this movie, which corresponds to Part II, is also a must-see movie.

To resolve the confusion of the world today, people all over the world must know the age of the God of Genesis and the age of the God who indicated the criteria to divide heaven and hell.

And now, in the 21st century, is the third descent—the age of El Cantare has begun.

The Laws of El Cantare will reveal the Genesis, the right way for humanity, and the mission of earthlings in the space age.

In times of difficulties, humanity shall know the appearance of the God of the Earth and His teachings.

This book is one of the new Bible or new Buddhist Scriptures. Whether you have this book or not will determine the course of your future.

Ryuho Okawa
Master & CEO of Happy Science Group
August 21, 2021

ABOUT THE AUTHOR

RYUHO OKAWA was born on July 7th 1956, in Tokushima, Japan. After graduating from the University of Tokyo with a law degree, he joined a Tokyo-based trading house. While working at its New York headquarters, he studied international finance at the Graduate Center of the City University of New York. In 1981, he attained Great Enlightenment and became aware that he is El Cantare with a mission to bring salvation to all humankind. In 1986, he established Happy Science. It now has members in over 160 countries across the world, with more than 700 branches and temples as well as 10,000 missionary houses around the world. The total number of lectures has exceeded 3,350 (of which more than 150 are in English) and over 2,900 books (of which more than 600 are Spiritual Interview Series) have been published, many of which are translated into 37 languages. Many of the books, including *The Laws of the Sun* have become best sellers or million sellers. To date, Happy Science has produced 23 movies. The original story and original concept were given by the Executive Producer Ryuho Okawa. Recent movie titles are *Beautiful Lure—A Modern Tale of "Painted Skin"* (live-action, May 2021), *Into the Dreams... and Horror Experiences* (live-action, August 2021), and *The Laws of the Universe - The Age of Elohim* (animation movie, October 2021). He has also composed the lyrics and music of over 450 songs, such as theme songs and featured songs of movies. Moreover, he is the Founder of Happy Science University and Happy Science Academy (Junior and Senior High School), Founder and President of the Happiness Realization Party, Founder and Honorary Headmaster of Happy Science Institute of Government and Management, Founder of IRH Press Co., Ltd., and the Chairperson of NEW STAR PRODUCTION Co., Ltd. and ARI Production Co., Ltd.

WHAT IS EL CANTARE?

El Cantare means "the Light of the Earth," and is the Supreme God of the Earth who has been guiding humankind since the beginning of Genesis. He is whom Jesus called Father and Muhammad called Allah, and is the Creator in Shintoism, *Ame-no-Mioya-Gami*. Different parts of El Cantare's core consciousness have descended to Earth in the past, once as Alpha and another as Elohim. His branch spirits, such as Shakyamuni Buddha and Hermes, have descended to Earth many times and helped to flourish many civilizations. To unite various religions and to integrate various fields of study in order to build a new civilization on Earth, a part of the core consciousness has descended to Earth as Master Ryuho Okawa.

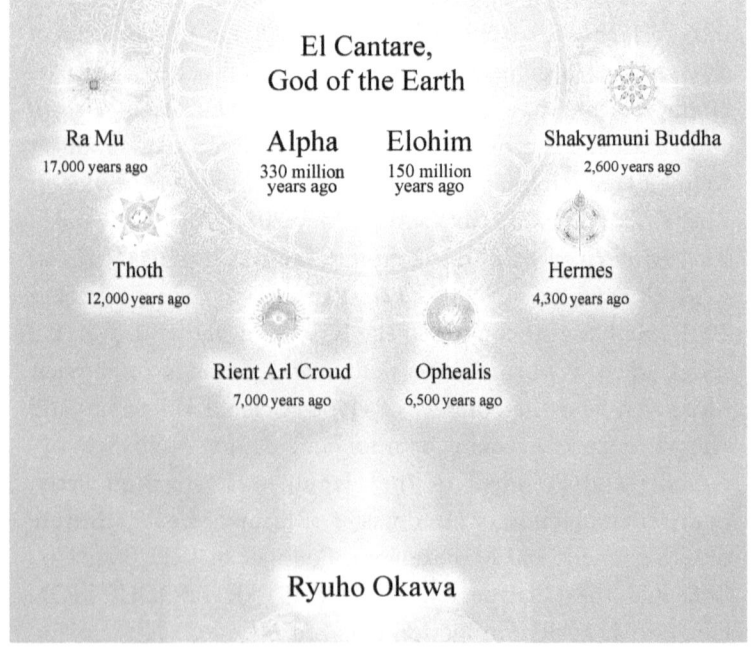

Alpha is a part of the core consciousness of El Cantare who descended to Earth around 330 million years ago. Alpha preached Earth's Truths to harmonize and unify Earth-born humans and space people who came from other planets.

Elohim is a part of El Cantare's core consciousness who descended to Earth around 150 million years ago. He gave wisdom, mainly on the differences of light and darkness, good and evil.

Shakyamuni Buddha was born as a prince into the Shakya Clan in India around 2,600 years ago. When he was 29 years old, he renounced the world and sought enlightenment. He later attained Great Enlightenment and founded Buddhism.

Hermes is one of the 12 Olympian gods in Greek mythology, but the spiritual Truth is that he taught the teachings of love and progress around 4,300 years ago that became the origin of the current Western civilization. He is a hero that truly existed.

Ophealis was born in Greece around 6,500 years ago and was the leader who took an expedition to as far as Egypt. He is the God of miracles, prosperity, and arts, and is known as Osiris in the Egyptian mythology.

Rient Arl Croud was born as a king of the ancient Incan Empire around 7,000 years ago and taught about the mysteries of the mind. In the heavenly world, he is responsible for the interactions that take place between various planets.

Thoth was an almighty leader who built the golden age of the Atlantic civilization around 12,000 years ago. In the Egyptian mythology, he is known as god Thoth.

Ra Mu was a leader who built the golden age of the civilization of Mu around 17,000 years ago. As a religious leader and a politician, he ruled by uniting religion and politics.

WHAT IS A SPIRITUAL MESSAGE?

We are all spiritual beings living on this earth. The following is the mechanism behind Master Ryuho Okawa's spiritual messages.

1 You are a spirit

People are born into this world to gain wisdom through various experiences and return to the other world when their lives end. We are all spirits and repeat this cycle in order to refine our souls.

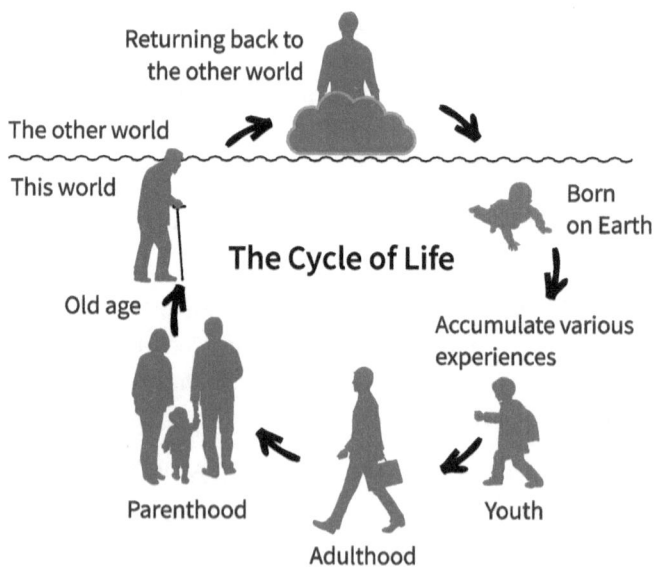

2 You have a guardian spirit

Guardian spirits are those who protect the people who are living on this earth. Each of us has a guardian spirit that watches over us and guides us from the other world. They were us in our past life, and are identical in how we think.

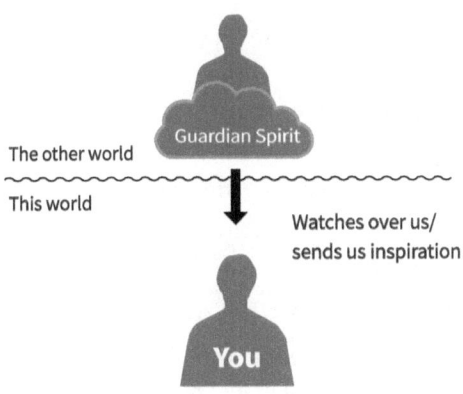

3 How spiritual messages work

Master Ryuho Okawa, through his enlightenment, is capable of summoning any spirit from anywhere in the world, including the spirit world.

Master Okawa's way of receiving spiritual messages is fundamentally different from that of other psychic mediums who undergo trances and are thereby completely taken over by the spirits they are channeling.

Master Okawa's attainment of a high level of enlightenment enables him to retain full control of his consciousness and body throughout the duration of the spiritual message. To allow the spirits to express their own thoughts and personalities freely, however, Master Okawa usually softens the dominancy of his consciousness. This way, he is able to keep his own philosophies out of the way and ensure that the spiritual messages are pure expressions of the spirits he is channeling.

Since guardian spirits think at the same subconscious level as the person living on earth, Master Okawa can summon the spirit and find out what the person on earth is actually thinking. If the person has already returned to the other world, the spirit can give messages to the people living on earth through Master Okawa.

Since 2009, more than 1,200 sessions of spiritual messages have been openly recorded by Master Okawa, and the majority of these have been published. Spiritual messages from the guardian spirits of people living today such as Donald Trump, former Japanese Prime Minister Shinzo Abe and Chinese President Xi Jinping, as well as spiritual messages sent from the spirit world by Jesus Christ, Muhammad, Thomas Edison, Mother Teresa, Steve Jobs and Nelson Mandela are just a tiny pack of spiritual messages that were published so far.

Domestically, in Japan, these spiritual messages are being read by a wide range of politicians and mass media, and the high-level contents of these books are delivering an impact even more on politics, news and public opinion. In recent years, there have been spiritual messages recorded in English, and English translations are being done on the spiritual messages given in Japanese. These have been published overseas, one after another, and have started to shake the world.

① The guardian spirit / spirit in the other world...

② Goes inside Master Okawa in this world

③ Master Okawa speaks the words of the guardian spirit / spirit

For more about spiritual messages and a complete list of books in the Spiritual Interview Series, visit okawabooks.com

ABOUT HAPPY SCIENCE

Happy Science is a global movement that empowers individuals to find purpose and spiritual happiness and to share that happiness with their families, societies, and the world. With more than 12 million members around the world, Happy Science aims to increase awareness of spiritual truths and expand our capacity for love, compassion, and joy so that together we can create the kind of world we all wish to live in.

Activities at Happy Science are based on the Principle of Happiness (Love, Wisdom, Self-Reflection, and Progress). This principle embraces worldwide philosophies and beliefs, transcending boundaries of culture and religions.

Love teaches us to give ourselves freely without expecting anything in return; it encompasses giving, nurturing, and forgiving.

Wisdom leads us to the insights of spiritual truths, and opens us to the true meaning of life and the will of God (the universe, the highest power, Buddha).

Self-Reflection brings a mindful, nonjudgmental lens to our thoughts and actions to help us find our truest selves—the essence of our souls—and deepen our connection to the highest power. It helps us attain a clean and peaceful mind and leads us to the right life path.

Progress emphasizes the positive, dynamic aspects of our spiritual growth—actions we can take to manifest and spread happiness around the world. It's a path that not only expands our soul growth, but also furthers the collective potential of the world we live in.

PROGRAMS AND EVENTS

The doors of Happy Science are open to all. We offer a variety of programs and events, including self-exploration and self-growth programs, spiritual seminars, meditation and contemplation sessions, study groups, and book events.

Our programs are designed to:
* Deepen your understanding of your purpose and meaning in life
* Improve your relationships and increase your capacity to love unconditionally
* Attain peace of mind, decrease anxiety and stress, and feel positive
* Gain deeper insights and a broader perspective on the world
* Learn how to overcome life's challenges
  ... and much more.

For more information, visit happy-science.org.

OUR ACTIVITIES

Happy Science does other various activities to provide support for those in need.

◆ You Are An Angel! General Incorporated Association

Happy Science has a volunteer network in Japan that encourages and supports children with disabilities as well as their parents and guardians.

◆ Never Mind School for Truancy

At 'Never Mind,' we support students who find it very challenging to attend schools in Japan. We also nurture their self-help spirit and power to rebound against obstacles in life based on Master Okawa's teachings and faith.

◆ "Prevention Against Suicide" Campaign since 2003

A nationwide campaign to reduce suicides; over 20,000 people commit suicide every year in Japan. "The Suicide Prevention Website-Words of Truth for You-" presents spiritual prescriptions for worries such as depression, lost love, extramarital affairs, bullying and work-related problems, thereby saving many lives.

◆ Support for Anti-bullying Campaigns

Happy Science provides support for a group of parents and guardians, Network to Protect Children from Bullying, a general incorporated foundation launched in Japan to end bullying, including those that can even be called a criminal offense. So far, the network received more than 5,000 cases and resolved 90% of them.

- The Golden Age Scholarship
  This scholarship is granted to students who can contribute greatly and bring a hopeful future to the world.

- Success No.1
  Buddha's Truth Afterschool Academy
  Happy Science has over 180 classrooms throughout Japan and in several cities around the world that focus on afterschool education for children. The education focuses on faith and morals in addition to supporting children's school studies.

- Angel Plan V
  For children under the age of kindergarten, Happy Science holds classes for nurturing healthy, positive, and creative boys and girls.

- Future Stars Training Department
  The Future Stars Training Department was founded within the Happy Science Media Division with the goal of nurturing talented individuals to become successful in the performing arts and entertainment industry.

- NEW STAR PRODUCTION Co., Ltd.
  ARI Production Co., Ltd.
  We have companies to nurture actors and actresses, artists, and vocalists. They are also involved in film production.

ABOUT HAPPINESS REALIZATION PARTY

The Happiness Realization Party (HRP) was founded in May 2009 by Master Ryuho Okawa as part of the Happy Science Group. HRP strives to improve the Japanese society, based on three basic political principles of "freedom, democracy, and faith," and let Japan promote individual and public happiness from Asia to the world as a leader nation.

1) Diplomacy and Security: Protecting Freedom, Democracy, and Faith of Japan and the World from China's Totalitarianism

Japan's current defense system is insufficient against China's expanding hegemony and the threat of North Korea's nuclear missiles. Japan, as the leader of Asia, must strengthen its defense power and promote strategic diplomacy together with the nations which share the values of freedom, democracy, and faith. Further, HRP aims to realize world peace under the leadership of Japan, the nation with the spirit of religious tolerance.

2) Economy: Early economic recovery through utilizing the "wisdom of the private sector"

Economy has been damaged severely by the novel coronavirus originated in China. Many companies have been forced into bankruptcy or out of business. What is needed for economic recovery now is not subsidies and regulations by the government, but policies which can utilize the "wisdom of the private sector."

For more information, visit en.hr-party.jp

HAPPY SCIENCE ACADEMY JUNIOR AND SENIOR HIGH SCHOOL

Happy Science Academy Junior and Senior High School is a boarding school founded with the goal of educating the future leaders of the world who can have a big vision, persevere, and take on new challenges.

Currently, there are two campuses in Japan; the Nasu Main Campus in Tochigi Prefecture, founded in 2010, and the Kansai Campus in Shiga Prefecture, founded in 2013.

Nasu Main Campus

Kansai Campus

 **HAPPY SCIENCE UNIVERSITY**

THE FOUNDING SPIRIT AND THE GOAL OF EDUCATION

Based on the founding philosophy of the university, "Exploration of happiness and the creation of a new civilization," education, research and studies will be provided to help students acquire deep understanding grounded in religious belief and advanced expertise with the objectives of producing "great talents of virtue" who can contribute in a broad-ranging way to serve Japan and the international society.

FACULTIES

Faculty of human happiness

Students in this faculty will pursue liberal arts from various perspectives with a multidisciplinary approach, explore and envision an ideal state of human beings and society.

Faculty of successful management

This faculty aims to realize successful management that helps organizations to create value and wealth for society and to contribute to the happiness and the development of management and employees as well as society as a whole.

Faculty of future creation

Students in this faculty study subjects such as political science, journalism, performing arts and artistic expression, and explore and present new political and cultural models based on truth, goodness and beauty.

Faculty of future industry

This faculty aims to nurture engineers who can resolve various issues facing modern civilization from a technological standpoint and contribute to the creation of new industries of the future.

CONTACT INFORMATION

Happy Science is a worldwide organization with faith centers around the globe. For a comprehensive list of centers, visit the worldwide directory at *happy-science.org*. The following are some of the many Happy Science locations:

UNITED STATES AND CANADA

New York
79 Franklin St., New York, NY 10013
Phone: 212-343-7972
Fax: 212-343-7973
Email: ny@happy-science.org
Website: happyscience-usa.org

New Jersey
725 River Rd, #102B, Edgewater, NJ 07020
Phone: 201-313-0127
Fax: 201-313-0120
Email: nj@happy-science.org
Website: happyscience-usa.org

Florida
5208 8th St., Zephyrhills, FL 33542
Phone: 813-715-0000
Fax: 813-715-0010
Email: florida@happy-science.org
Website: happyscience-usa.org

Atlanta
1874 Piedmont Ave., NE Suite 360-C
Atlanta, GA 30324
Phone: 404-892-7770
Email: atlanta@happy-science.org
Website: happyscience-usa.org

San Francisco
525 Clinton St.
Redwood City, CA 94062
Phone & Fax: 650-363-2777
Email: sf@happy-science.org
Website: happyscience-usa.org

Los Angeles
1590 E. Del Mar Blvd., Pasadena, CA 91106
Phone: 626-395-7775
Fax: 626-395-7776
Email: la@happy-science.org
Website: happyscience-usa.org

Orange County
10231 Slater Ave., #204
Fountain Valley, CA 92708
Phone: 714-659-1501
Email: oc@happy-science.org
Website: happyscience-usa.org

San Diego
7841 Balboa Ave., Suite #202
San Diego, CA 92111
Phone: 626-395-7775
Fax: 626-395-7776
E-mail: sandiego@happy-science.org
Website: happyscience-usa.org

Hawaii
Phone: 808-591-9772
Fax: 808-591-9776
Email: hi@happy-science.org
Website: happyscience-usa.org

Kauai
3343 Kanakolu Street, Suite 5
Lihue, HI 96766, U.S.A.
Phone: 808-822-7007
Fax: 808-822-6007
Email: kauai-hi@happy-science.org
Website: happyscience-usa.org

Toronto
845 The Queensway
Etobicoke ON M8Z 1N6 Canada
Phone: 1-416-901-3747
Email: toronto@happy-science.org
Website: happy-science.ca

Vancouver
#201-2607 East 49th Avenue
Vancouver, BC, V5S 1J9, Canada
Phone: 1-604-437-7735
Fax: 1-604-437-7764
Email: vancouver@happy-science.org
Website: happy-science.ca

INTERNATIONAL

Tokyo
1-6-7 Togoshi, Shinagawa
Tokyo, 142-0041 Japan
Phone: 81-3-6384-5770
Fax: 81-3-6384-5776
Email: tokyo@happy-science.org
Website: happy-science.org

Seoul
74, Sadang-ro 27-gil,
Dongjak-gu, Seoul, Korea
Phone: 82-2-3478-8777
Fax: 82-2-3478-9777
Email: korea@happy-science.org
Website: happyscience-korea.org

London
3 Margaret St.
London,W1W 8RE United Kingdom
Phone: 44-20-7323-9255
Fax: 44-20-7323-9344
Email: eu@happy-science.org
Website: happyscience-uk.org

Taipei
No. 89, Lane 155, Dunhua N. Road
Songshan District, Taipei City 105, Taiwan
Phone: 886-2-2719-9377
Fax: 886-2-2719-5570
Email: taiwan@happy-science.org
Website: happyscience-tw.org

Sydney
516 Pacific Hwy, Lane Cove North,
NSW 2066, Australia
Phone: 61-2-9411-2877
Fax: 61-2-9411-2822
Email: sydney@happy-science.org

Malaysia
No 22A, Block 2, Jalil Link Jalan Jalil
Jaya 2, Bukit Jalil 57000, Kuala Lumpur, Malaysia
Phone: 60-3-8998-7877
Fax: 60-3-8998-7977
Email: malaysia@happy-science.org
Website: happyscience.org.my

Brazil Headquarters
Rua. Domingos de Morais 1154,
Vila Mariana, Sao Paulo SP
CEP 04010-100, Brazil
Phone: 55-11-5088-3800
Email: sp@happy-science.org
Website: happyscience.com.br

Nepal
Kathmandu Metropolitan City Ward
No. 15,
Ring Road, Kimdol,
Sitapaila Kathmandu, Nepal
Phone: 97-714-272931
Email: nepal@happy-science.org

Jundiai
Rua Congo, 447, Jd. Bonfiglioli
Jundiai-CEP, 13207-340
Phone: 55-11-4587-5952
Email: jundiai@happy-science.org

Uganda
Plot 877 Rubaga Road, Kampala
P.O. Box 34130, Kampala, Uganda
Phone: 256-79-4682-121
Email: uganda@happy-science.org
Website: happyscience-uganda.org

ABOUT IRH PRESS

IRH Press Co., Ltd., based in Tokyo, was founded in 1987 as a publishing division of Happy Science. IRH Press publishes religious and spiritual books, journals, magazines and also operates broadcast and film production enterprises. For more information, visit *okawabooks.com*.

Follow us on:
Facebook: Okawa Books   Twitter: Okawa Books
Goodreads: Ryuho Okawa   Instagram: OkawaBooks
Pinterest: Okawa Books

--- **NEWSLETTER** ---

To receive book related news, promotions and events, please subscribe to our newsletter below.

https://okawabooks.us11.list-manage.com/subscribe?u=1fc70960eefd92668052ab7f8&id=2fbd8150ef

--- **MEDIA** ---

OKAWA BOOK CLUB

A conversation about Ryuho Okawa's titles, topics ranging from self-help, current affairs, spirituality and religions.

Available at iTunes, Spotify and Amazon Music.

Apple iTunes:
https://podcasts.apple.com/us/podcast/okawa-book-club/id1527893043

Spotify:
https://open.spotify.com/show/09mpgX2iJ6stVm4eBRdo2b

Amazon Music:
https://music.amazon.com/podcasts/7b759f24-ff72-4523-bfee-24f48294998f/Okawa-Book-Club

BOOKS BY RYUHO OKAWA

RYUHO OKAWA'S LAWS SERIES

The Laws Series is an annual volume of books that are mainly comprised of Ryuho Okawa's lectures that function as universal guidance to all people. They are of various topics that were given in accordance with the changes that each year brings. *The Laws of the Sun*, the first publication of the laws series, ranked in the annual best-selling list in Japan in 1994. Since, the laws series' titles have ranked in the annual best-selling list every year for more than two decades, setting socio-cultural trends in Japan and around the world.

The 27th Laws Series
THE LAWS OF SECRET

Awaken to This New World and Change Your Life

Paperback • 248 pages • $16.95
ISBN: 978-1-942125-81-5

Our physical world coexists with the multi-dimensional spirit world and we are constantly interacting with some kind of spiritual energy, whether positive or negative, without consciously realizing it. This book reveals how our lives are affected by invisible influences, including the spiritual reasons behind influenza, the novel coronavirus infection, and other illnesses.

The new view of the world in this book will inspire you to change your life in a better direction, and to become someone who can give hope and courage to others in this age of confusion.

For a complete list of books, visit okawabooks.com

THE TRILOGY

The first three volumes of the Laws Series, *The Laws of the Sun*, *The Golden Laws*, and *The Nine Dimensions* make a trilogy that completes the basic framework of the teachings of God's Truths. *The Laws of the Sun* discusses the structure of God's Laws, *The Golden Laws* expounds on the doctrine of time, and *The Nine Dimensions* reveals the nature of space.

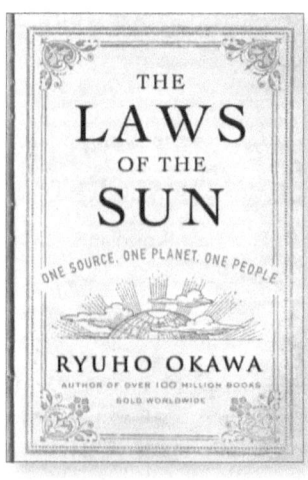

THE LAWS OF THE SUN

ONE SOURCE, ONE PLANET, ONE PEOPLE

Paperback • 288 pages • $15.95
ISBN: 978-1-942125-43-3

IMAGINE IF YOU COULD ASK GOD why He created this world and what spiritual laws He used to shape us—and everything around us. If we could understand His designs and intentions, we could discover what our goals in life should be and whether our actions move us closer to those goals or farther away.

At a young age, a spiritual calling prompted Ryuho Okawa to outline what he innately understood to be universal truths for all humankind. In *The Laws of the Sun*, Okawa outlines these laws of the universe and provides a road map for living one's life with greater purpose and meaning.

In this powerful book, Ryuho Okawa reveals the transcendent nature of consciousness and the secrets of our multidimensional universe and our place in it. By understanding the different stages of love and following the Buddhist Eightfold Path, he believes we can speed up our eternal process of development. *The Laws of the Sun* shows the way to realize true happiness—a happiness that continues from this world through the other.

For a complete list of books, visit <u>okawabooks.com</u>

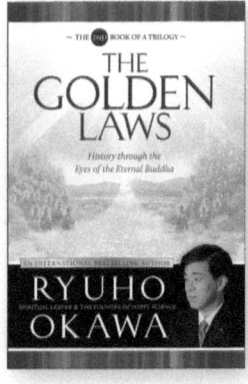

THE GOLDEN LAWS
HISTORY THROUGH THE EYES OF THE ETERNAL BUDDHA

Paperback • 201 pages • $14.95
ISBN: 978-1-941779-81-1

Throughout history, Great Guiding Spirits have been present on Earth in both the East and the West at crucial points in human history to further our spiritual development. *The Golden Laws* reveals how Divine Plan has been unfolding on Earth, and outlines 5,000 years of the secret history of humankind. Once we understand the true course of history, through past, present and into the future, we cannot help but become aware of the significance of our spiritual mission in the present age.

THE NINE DIMENSIONS
UNVEILING THE LAWS OF ETERNITY

Paperback • 168 pages • $15.95
ISBN: 978-0-982698-56-3

This book is a window into the mind of our loving God, who designed this world and the vast, wondrous world of our afterlife as a school with many levels through which our souls learn and grow. When the religions and cultures of the world discover the truth of their common spiritual origin, they will be inspired to accept their differences, come together under faith in God, and build an era of harmony and peaceful progress on Earth.

For a complete list of books, visit okawabooks.com

LAWS SERIES

THE LAWS OF HOPE
THE LIGHT IS HERE

Paperback • 224 pages • $16.95
ISBN:978-1-942125-76-1

This book provides ways to bring light and hope to ourselves through our own efforts, even in the midst of sufferings and adversities. Inspired by a wish to bring happiness, success, and hope to humanity, Okawa shows us how to look at and think about our lives and circumstances. By making efforts in your current circumstances, you can fulfill your mission to shed light on yourself and those around you.

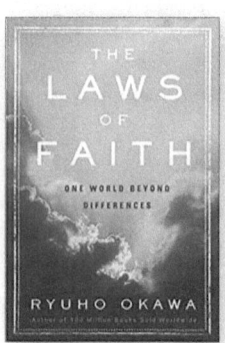

THE LAWS OF FAITH
ONE WORLD BEYOND DIFFERENCES

Paperback • 208 pages • $15.95
ISBN: 978-1-942125-34-1

Ryuho Okawa preaches at the core of a new universal religion from various angles while integrating logical and spiritual viewpoints in mind with current world situations. This book offers us the key to accept diversities beyond differences in ethnicity, religion, race, gender, descent, and so on, harmonize the individuals and nations and create a world filled with peace and prosperity.

THE LAWS OF HAPPINESS
LOVE, WISDOM, SELF-REFLECTION AND PROGRESS

Paperback • 264 pages • $16.95
ISBN: 978-1-942125-70-9

What is happiness? In this book, Ryuho Okawa explains that happiness is not found outside us; it's found within us, in how we think, how we look at our lives in this world, what we believe in, and how we devote our hearts to the work we do. Even as we go through suffering and unfavorable circumstances, we can always shift our mindset and become happier by simply *giving love* instead of *taking love*.

For a complete list of books, visit okawabooks.com

BOOKS ON THE TRUTH OF THE SPIRIT WORLD

ROJIN, BUDDHA'S MYSTICAL POWER

ITS ULTIMATE ATTAINMENT IN TODAY'S WORLD

Paperback • 224 pages • $16.95
ISBN: 978-1-942125-82-2

In this book, Ryuho Okawa has redefined the traditional Buddhist term *Rojin* and explained that in modern society it means the following: the ability for individuals with great spiritual powers to live in the world as people with common sense while using their abilities to the optimal level. This book will unravel the mystery of the mind and lead you to the path to enlightenment.

THE ESSENCE OF BUDDHA

THE PATH TO ENLIGHTENMENT

Paperback • 208 pages • $14.95
ISBN: 978-1-942125-06-8

In this book, Ryuho Okawa imparts in simple and accessible language his wisdom about the essence of Shakyamuni Buddha's philosophy of life and enlightenment-teachings that have been inspiring people all over the world for over 2,500 years. By offering a new perspective on core Buddhist thoughts, Okawa brings these teachings to life for modern people. This book distills a way of life that anyone can practice to achieve a life of self-growth, compassionate living, and true happiness.

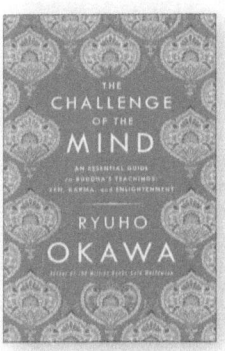

THE CHALLENGE OF THE MIND

AN ESSENTIAL GUIDE TO BUDDHA'S TEACHINGS: ZEN, KARMA AND ENLIGHTENMENT

Paperback • 208 pages • $16.95
ISBN: 978-1-942125-45-7

In this book, Ryuho Okawa explains essential Buddhist tenets and how to put them into practice. Enlightenment is not just an abstract idea but one that everyone can experience to some extent. Okawa offers a solid basis of reason and intellectual understanding to Buddhist concepts. By applying these basic principles to our lives, we can direct our minds to higher ideals and create a bright future for ourselves and others.

For a complete list of books, visit okawabooks.com

MOVIE "THE LAWS OF THE UNIVERSE - THE AGE OF ELOHIM" RELATED BOOKS

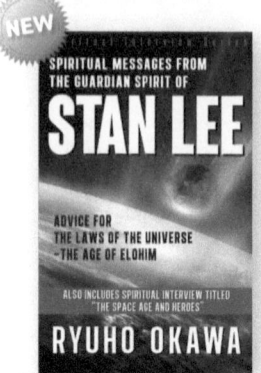

SPIRITUAL MESSAGES FROM THE GUARDIAN SPIRIT OF STAN LEE

ADVICE FOR *THE LAWS OF THE UNIVERSE - THE AGE OF ELOHIM*

Paperback • 200 pages • $11.95
ISBN: 978-1-943928-16-3

To seek advice on the plot for the movie *The Laws of the Universe - The Age of Elohim*, Okawa summoned the guardian spirit of Stan Lee, the father of Marvel Comics heroes. The guardian spirit of Stan Lee tells how he comes up with the heroes, and gives his insights on the kind of heroes that humans need in the coming Space Age.

SPIRITUAL INTERVIEWS WITH THE GUARDIAN SPIRIT OF GEORGE LUCAS AND THE SPIRIT OF CARRIE FISHER

AWAKENING MESSAGES TO THE SPACE AGE

Paperback • 154 pages • $11.95
ISBN: 978-1943928-14-9

In the world today, a large totalitarian nation is aiming to take control of the world, while small democratic powers are trying to resist its attack. By reading this book, you will realize that similar battles were already happening in outer space, and that the Star Wars Series is a saga based on the real-life stories.

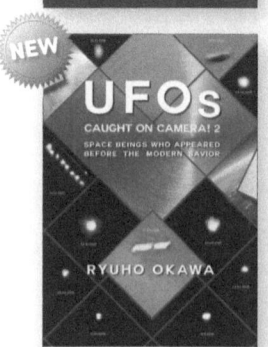

UFOS CAUGHT ON CAMERA! 2

SPACE BEINGS WHO APPEARED BEFORE THE MODERN SAVIOR

Paperback • 129 pages • $18.95
ISBN: 978-1-943928-15-6

UFOs Caught on Camera, employs Okawa's honed spiritual and psychic ability to gather unprecedented information such as vivid details of spacecraft configuration, the sector of origin, passenger description, and observable sentiment regarding Earth and its inhabitants. Includes photos of more than 50 types of UFOs and telepathic conversations with space beings.

For a complete list of books, visit okawabooks.com

MESSAGES FROM SPACE BEINGS

R. A. GOAL'S WORDS FOR THE FUTURE
MESSAGES FROM A SPACE BEING
TO THE PEOPLE OF EARTH

Paperback • 174 pages • $11.95
ISBN: 978-1-943928-10-1

R. A. Goal, a certified messiah from Planet Andalucia Beta in Ursa Minor, gives humans on Earth three predictions for 2021. They include the prospect of the novel coronavirus pandemic, the outlook of economic crisis, and the risk of war. But the hope is that Savior is now born on Earth to overcome any bad predictions. Now is the time to open our hearts and listen to the words from R. A. Goal.

THE TRUE HEART OF YAIDRON
GUIDELINES FOR HUMANKIND SUFFERING FROM THE CORONAVIRUS

Paperback • 144 pages • $11.95
ISBN: 978-1-943928-04-0

What are the real cause and evil schemes behind the worldwide coronavirus crisis? Out of compassion, this book reveals truths about the all-out global war now being waged by the evil power in East Asia that's destroying the power of the people. Discover the movement that's trying to bring together the powers of the West, India, and Asia by the belief of "With Savior," to save humankind and create the new golden future of Earth.

WITH SAVIOR
MESSAGES FROM SPACE BEING YAIDRON

Paperback • 232 pages • $13.95
ISBN: 978-1-943869-94-7

The human race is now faced with multiple unprecedented crises. Perhaps God is warning us humans to reconsider our materialistic and arrogant ways. Fortunately, God has sent us a savior, who is now teaching us to repent and showing us the path we should choose. In this book, space being Yaidron sends his warnings and messages of hope.

For a complete list of books, visit okawabooks.com

CONSIDERING THE FUTURE OF THE WORLD

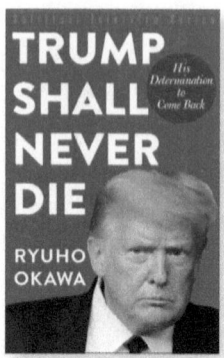

TRUMP SHALL NEVER DIE
HIS DETERMINATION TO COME BACK

Paperback • 206 pages • $11.95
ISBN: 978-1-943928-08-8

This book unveiled Mr. Donald Trump's true thoughts never reported by the media through spiritual interview with the guardian spirit of him. The topics include the "madness" found in GAFA and the mainstream media, Mr. Trump's views on the coronavirus vaccine and global warming, and the true aim of "Make America Great Again."

THE XI JINPING THOUGHT NOW

Paperback • 212 pages • $13.95
ISBN: 978-1-943928-05-7

With the launch of Biden administration in the U.S. and the 100th anniversary of the founding of the Chinese Communist Party approaching, China has been expanding its military threat and reinforcing its influence over the world. What urges China to seek global hegemony? This book unveils the "dark being" behind the Xi Jinping Thought.

HOW TO SURVIVE THE CORONAVIRUS RECESSION

Paperback • 171 pages • $14.95
ISBN: 978-1-943869-97-8

From the perspectives of both economics and health, this book delves into how you can survive the coronavirus recession. As taught by the author Ryuho Okawa, there is a strong relationship between your spiritual health and immunity, and he demonstrates the mindset you should have as well as introduces a very effective meditation that you can do to truly strengthen your immunity.

For a complete list of books, visit okawabooks.com

RECOMMENDED SPIRITUAL MESSAGES

JOHN LENNON'S MESSAGE FROM HEAVEN

ON THE SPIRIT OF LOVE AND PEACE, MUSIC, AND THE INCREDIBLE SECRET OF HIS SOUL

Paperback • 310 pages • $13.95
ISBN: 978-1-943869-78-7

John Lennon's Message from Heaven is a compilation of his spiritual message held in three separate parts. He speaks his real thoughts and feelings on many topics regarding the world's current and past conditions, and key aspects of the life he lived on Earth.

SPIRITUAL INTERVIEW WITH BRUCE LEE

THE RESURRECTION OF THE DRAGON

Paperback • 113 pages • $9.95
ISBN: 978-1-943869-34-3

Here, we present you, martial artists and Bruce Lee fans all over the world who respect him even after his death over 40 years ago, the truth revealed by the "Dragon" who is still fighting evil in the Spirit World. He speaks a lot about his own kung fu philosophy that he had deepened further after his death, as well as the truth of his young death and the mission of his soul.

THE SHAPE OF THINGS IN 2100

H. G. WELLS PREDICTS THE FUTURE OF THE WORLD

Paperback • 176 pages • $14.95
ISBN: 978-1-941779-37-8

What does H. G. Wells see for our future today? What was the nature of the crisis and hope he predicted in his novel, The Shape of Things to Come? His answers to these questions reveal the importance of bringing change to our world today to build a positive future.

For a complete list of books, visit okawabooks.com

THE LAWS OF GREAT ENLIGHTENMENT
Always Walk with Buddha

UFOS CAUGHT ON CAMERA!
A Spiritual Investigation on Videos and Photos
of the Luminous Objects Visiting Earth

THE LAWS OF SUCCESS
A Spiritual Guide to Turning Your Hopes into Reality

THE POWER OF BASICS
Introduction to Modern Zen Life of Calm,
Spirituality and Success

WORRY-FREE LIVING
Let Go of Stress and Live in Peace and Happiness

THE STRONG MIND
The Art of Building the Inner Strength
to Overcome Life's Difficulties

INVINCIBLE THINKING
An Essential Guide for a Lifetime of
Growth, Success, and Triumph

THINK BIG!
Be Positive and Be Brave to Achieve Your Dreams

CHANGE YOUR LIFE, CHANGE THE WORLD
A Spiritual Guide to Living Now

For a complete list of books, visit okawabooks.com

MUSIC BY RYUHO OKAWA

THE THUNDER
a composition for repelling the Coronavirus

We have been granted this music from our Lord. It will repel away the novel Coronavirus originated in China. Experience this magnificent powerful music.

Search on YouTube

`the thunder coronavirus` 🔍   for a short ad!

THE EXORCISM
prayer music for repelling Lost Spirits

Feel the divine vibrations of this Japanese and Western exorcising symphony to banish all evil possessions you suffer from and to purify your space!

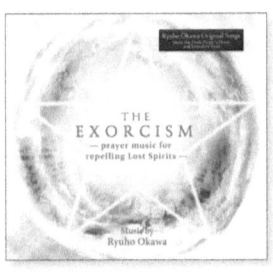

Search on YouTube

`the exorcism repelling` 🔍   for a short ad!

Download from **Listen now today!** **Spotify** **iTunes** **Amazon**

CD available at amazon.com, and Happy Science locations worldwide

WITH SAVIOR

English version

"Come what may, you shall expect your future"

This is the message of hope to the modern people who are living in the midst of the Coronavirus pandemic, natural disasters, economic depression, and other various crises.

Search on YouTube `with savior`   for a short ad!

THE WATER REVOLUTION

English and Chinese version

"Power to the People!"

For the truth and happiness of the 1.4 billion people in China who have no freedom. Love, justice, and sacred rage of God are on this melody that will give you courage to fight to bring peace.

Search on YouTube `the water revolution`   for a short ad!

CD available at amazon.com, and Happy Science locations worldwide

Download from 🎧 **Listen now today!**
Spotify   iTunes   Amazon

www.ingramcontent.com/pod-product-compliance
Lightning Source LLC
Chambersburg PA
CBHW030152100526
44592CB00009B/242